AF605773

AROUND AND ABOUT

AOTEAROA

Published in 2023 by David Bateman Ltd
Unit 2/5 Workspace Drive, Hobsonville, Auckland 0618, New Zealand
www.batemanbooks.co.nz

ISBN 978-1-77689-058-3

Illustrations: Dave Gunson
Cover design: Alice Bell and Dave Gunson
Book design: Alice Bell and Dave Gunson
Printed in China by Toppan Leefung Printing Ltd

AROUND AND ABOUT AOTEAROA

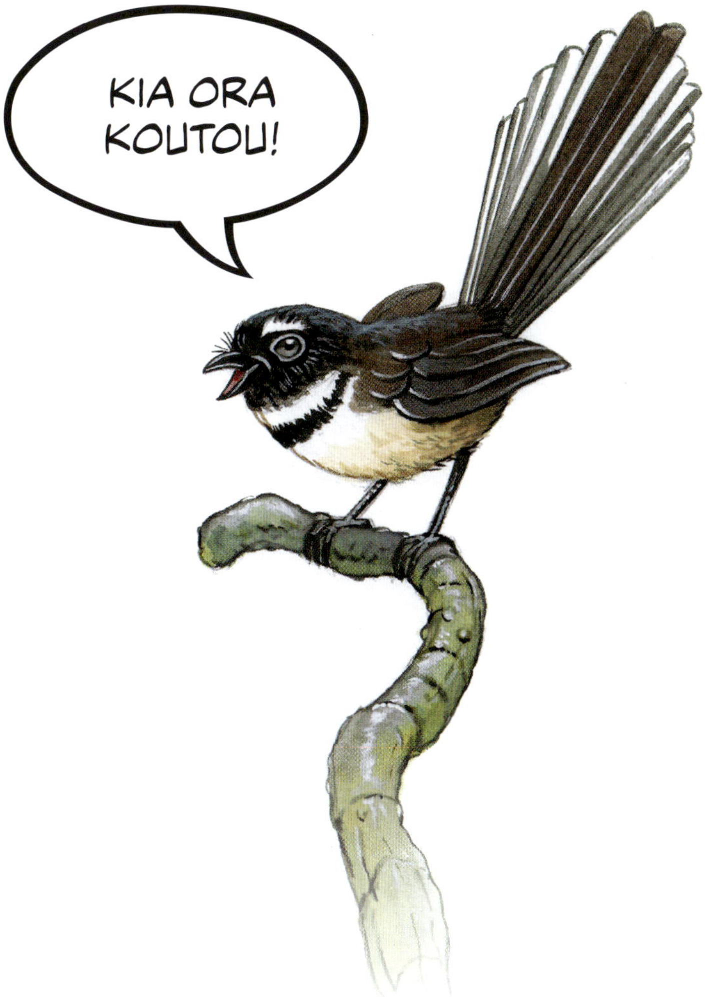

KIA ORA
KOUTOU!

DAVE GUNSON

CONTENTS

INTRODUCTION

So, what's this book all about?

Well, it covers a lot of the interesting stuff around and about Aotearoa, aka New Zealand . . . some of it you really should know, and there's some you might already know something about but not the full story, and there's plenty of stuff that you probably didn't know that you didn't know!

There's lots of important and helpful information, together with heaps of weird, odd, funny and amazing facts, figures, bits and pieces of history, events and happenings all mixed in . . . stuff that all Aotearoans (is that a word? Well . . . it is now!) will be fascinated to learn about. And plenty of fun on the way, too.

It's a quirky tiki tour around and about Aotearoa, past and present, and there's even a timeline of interesting events at the back of the book.

Heaps of good stuff!

Dave Gunson

SO, WHERE DID IT ALL BEGIN?

Aotearoa had its beginnings hundreds of millions of years ago. Back in those times, planet Earth had just two great super-continents — Laurasia in the north, and Gondwanaland in the south.

Over long periods of time, the movements of the tectonic plates that make up the Earth's crust (see page 24) began to pull Gondwanaland apart into smaller pieces — which eventually became India, Antarctica, South America, Africa, Australia and even parts of Europe and the Middle East. In one corner of Gondwanaland — between 120 and 80 million years ago — a small chunk of land was slowly drawn away into what we now know as the Pacific Ocean. This piece of land changed size and shape many times, and sometimes — due to falling and rising water levels as a result of cooling and warming periods in the Earth's history — became variously a large landmass or a series of small islands, and at one point almost disappeared under the waves completely. Luckily for us, it managed to survive.

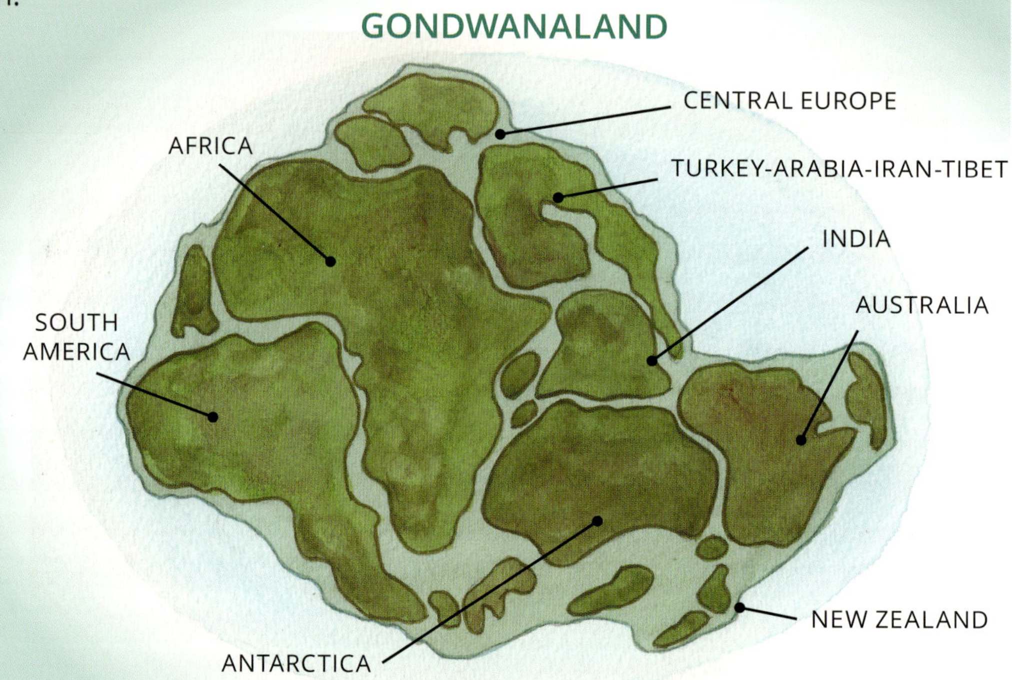

Of course, New Zealand didn't just unclip from Gondwanaland and float off; it took millions of years for the great continental plates to pull Gondwanaland apart and draw the 'pieces' away.

The mass of land that was drawn away from Gondwanaland has been mostly under water since that time, with its higher parts appearing above the waves as islands, large and small. About 15 times larger than New Zealand itself, it stretches from New Caledonia and Norfolk Island to almost halfway to Antarctica, and is now generally known as the submerged continent of Zealandia.

Its te reo Māori name is Te Riu-a-Māui, which means the hills, valleys and plains of Māui.

FROM DINOSAURS TO MOA

Dinosaurs, reptiles, insects and plants were all long established throughout Gondwanaland as the continent of Zealandia finally separated. And many of them came along for the ride. For tens of millions of years they all lived and developed here in total isolation from the rest of the world, before the great extinctions at the end of the Cretaceous period about 65 million years ago.

We've discovered a great deal of fossil evidence of New Zealand's ancient life over the years. The earliest animal fossils in Aotearoa rocks — about 500 million years old — are those of many species of tiny trilobites, discovered at Cobb Valley, near Nelson. These 2–4-centimetre-long creatures probably lived as modern crabs do today, in shallow coastal waters where they would roam for small prey and food scraps.

Giant reptiles ruled the seas around us. Plesiosaurs up to 7 metres long chased and took their prey with a frightful bite of 170 teeth, and the longer-necked elasmosaurs — over 9 metres long — joined the hunt, too. Giant mosasaurs (with extra rows of teeth in the roofs of their mouths) and pliosaurs (with the biggest-known jaws of any predator) hunted throughout our seas. The fossils of several species of these giant beasts have been found around the country.

HEY, THAT'S NOT FAIR!

There were also giants in the air. Pterosaurs (with wingspans of 3–4 metres) hunted around the coast and skimmed the waves to snatch up squid and fish. And even insects got in on the act . . . giant dragonflies (with wingspans equalling modern seagulls) hunted down other flying insects in aerial attacks.

And there were plenty of impressive animals on land, too. Fossil hunters have revealed the presence of many types of dinosaur. There were armoured ankylosaurs, herds of plant-eating hypsilophodonts, ornithomimosaurs, sauropods, ceratosaurs, huge allosaurs (distant relatives of dinosaurs like the T-rex) down to the tiny compsognathus — featured in *The Lost World: Jurassic Park.*

THE DAY AN ALLOSAUR MET A COMPSOGNATHUS FOR THE VERY FIRST TIME.

Although dinosaurs and many other animals became extinct some 65 million years ago, some managed to survive, and thrive. Ancestors of the tuatara had evolved long before the dinosaurs came to dominate the landscape and have remained almost unchanged to the present day (see page 34).

Crocodiles and alligators, too, survived the great extinctions, and up until about 20 million years ago, New Zealand's own crocodile — about 3–5 metres long — hunted for prey in rivers and swamps.

Giants continued to evolve, especially our birds. The fossil remains of several species of giant penguin have been found — each one bigger than the one previously discovered! The largest one so far found once stood 1.6 metres in height and weighed about 80 kilograms.

There were giant kākāpō — the largest parrots ever to have existed — standing a metre tall, and weighing about 7 kilograms. And scuttling away from their big feet was the giant gecko — kawekaweau — easily twice the size of today's species.

And, of course, there were moa. There were several species, adapted to living in different environments. The largest of all was the female giant moa; it could measure about 2 metres at shoulder height (up to 3 metres with its head held up), and weigh about 250–350 kilograms.

And it takes a giant to hunt a giant — the extinct New Zealand giant eagle had talons the size of a tiger's, weighed about 13 kilograms and had a wingspan of almost 3 metres . . . it was the largest bird of prey the world has ever known. It kept a watch from a high perch, ready to swoop down on those large flightless birds as they crossed open ground . . . those that hadn't already been caught and eaten by early Māori settlers, that is.

MĀORI SETTLERS

Polynesia was gradually settled over thousands of years by voyagers from the west, exploring and moving slowly through the chains of large and small islands into the lower Pacific Ocean. These travellers settled in Samoa, Tonga, the Cook Islands and so on. Further voyages took them north to Hawaii, and about 700 years ago explorers — the first Māori — came south to New Zealand. Some of these early travellers moved on to the Chatham Islands, and became the people we know as Moriori.

Settlements grew as more and more Māori arrived, and iwi/tribal territories became established throughout most of the North Island, and later in the South Island.

These first settlers brought food plants with them, such as kūmara and taro, and animals too — kurī (Polynesian dog) and kiore (Polynesian rat). The kurī became extinct in the 1860s, but the kiore still survives in remote places and on some islands.

Iwi cleared land for gardens and crops, fished the rivers and coasts, and hunted the moa and other flightless birds. Fortified villages — pā — were built, usually on headlands and hilltops. As these communities developed, they both formed alliances and warred with other iwi.

Art and culture grew, with distinctive crafts and styles of architecture and carving. Music and dance were all essential parts of Māori culture. Kite-flying and puppetry, too.

The word 'Polynesia' was first used in 1756, by Charles de Brosses. The word comes from the Greek; *poly* many, *nesos* island — many islands.

There were many 'waves' of settlement by Māori, and as the great double-hulled canoes arrived at different localities around the coast, and at different times, so these places became the original founding lands of each developing iwi. There have been many shifts in the territories of iwi and hapū (sub-tribes), and although many borders between territories — or rohe — can be quite flexible, this map shows the general arrangement of modern iwi.

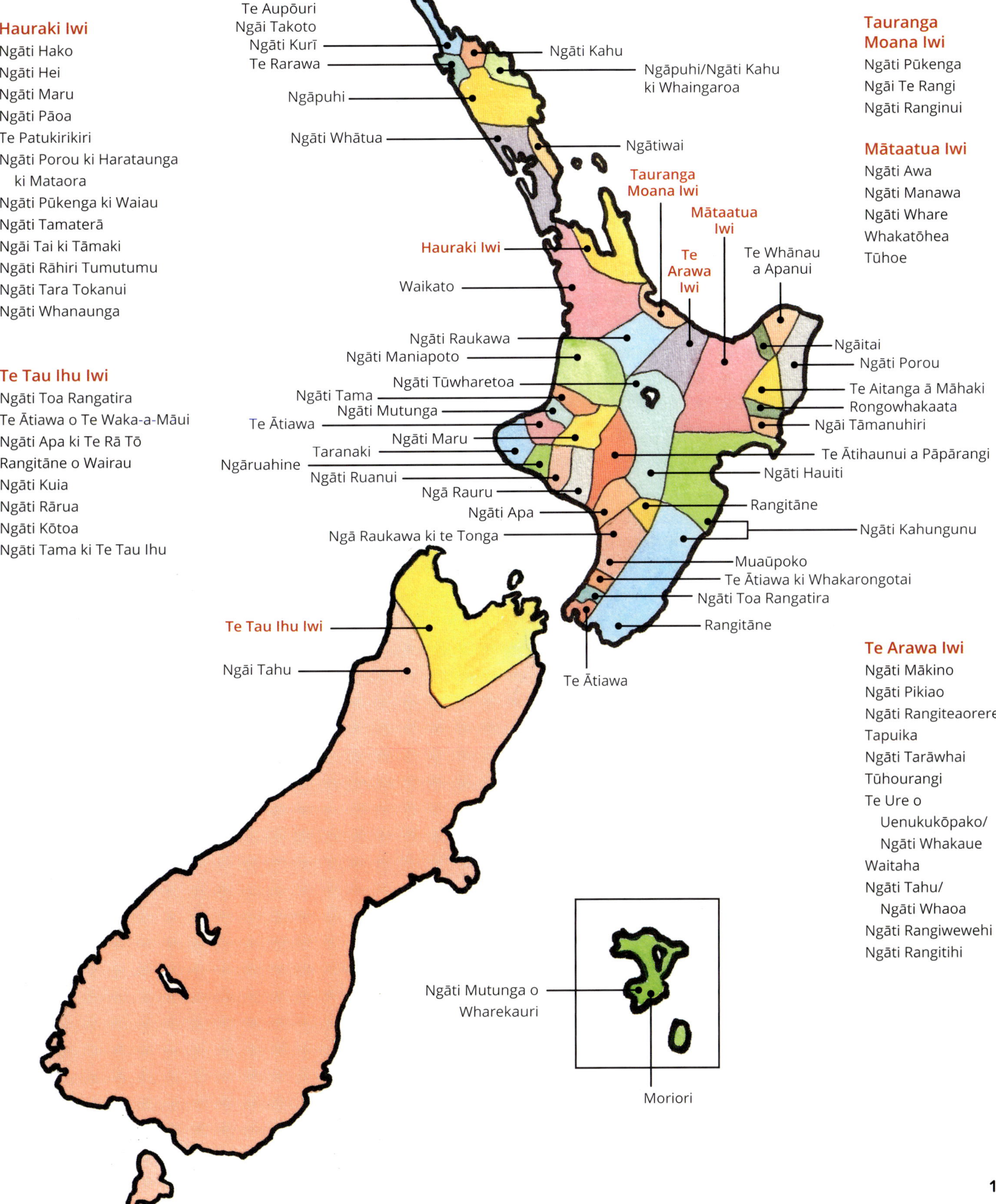

EUROPEAN SETTLERS

Māori had been well established through most of the country for hundreds of years before Europeans arrived on these islands.

Explorers, such as Tasman (1642), De Surville (1769) and Du Fresne (1772) mapped parts of the country, and made themselves known to Māori — sometimes the encounters were welcome and successful, and sometimes not.

It was during and immediately after Captain James Cook's visits here in 1769–70, 1773 and 1777 that Europeans came here in greater numbers. Traders, whalers and sealers were all quick to see new opportunities. Missionaries and new settlers arrived, and there was increased trade with Māori, who welcomed the innovations that Europeans brought — new crops, foodstuffs, farming methods and metal tools.

In the 1800s, the first mail-order catalogues appeared, which meant that goods could be selected and ordered direct from overseas merchants and retailers. But having to rely on sailing ships, and later steam ships, for communication meant orders could take over a year to arrive.

But Europeans brought many other things too . . . more species of rat, diseases that were previously unknown here, such as influenza and measles, and they brought guns.

Northern Māori were the first to trade flax and other products for muskets, and — now armed with modern weapons — set off to settle old grievances with other iwi.

Other iwi — such as Waikato — followed suit, and soon various North Island iwi were equipped, and many wars followed. From about 1818 to 1840 some 20,000 warriors were killed in battle.

Both Māori and Pākehā realised that this situation couldn't continue, and the Treaty of Waitangi — Tiriti o Waitangi — was drawn up to give Māori the rights and privileges of British subjects, and help to control the sale of land and encourage safe trading. There were two versions; one in English, and one in Māori, and this has led to many disputes ever since over the actual intent and meaning of each one. Over 500 Māori signed the Māori language version, but only 39 signed the English language version. Some Māori didn't agree to sign either document.

It didn't take long before disputes over land purchases arose, and there were many land confiscations by the government. Māori again took up arms, and between 1845 and 1872 — a period known as the New Zealand Land Wars — there were many battles between British and Māori forces, with victories and losses on both sides, before calmer days returned.

THE HAKA

A haka — the name means 'fiery breath' — can be performed as a show of defiance, respect and challenge. There are many different haka, but the most famous and most often used is one written by Te Rauparaha, the Ngāti Toa chief. When being sought by his enemies from Ngāti Maniapoto and Waikato, a friendly chief hid him in his kūmara pit. He wrote 'Ka Mate' in celebration of his escape.

'Ka Mate' is a haka taparahi — a ceremonial haka, and the All Blacks often use this haka to challenge the opposition before the start of a game.

All haka involve pukana — the vigorous use of facial expression, such as protruding tongues and glaring eyes.

The haka leader usually exhorts and directs the haka party with this call . . .

Ringa pakia
Slap your hands against your thighs
Uma tiriha
Stick out your chest
Turi whatia
Bend your knees
Hope whai ake
Let your hip follow
Waewae takahia kia kino
Stamp your feet as hard as you can

Then all perform the haka.

Ka mate! Ka mate! Ka ora! Ka ora!
I die! I die! I live! I live!
Ka mate! Ka mate! Ka ora! Ka ora!
I die! I die! I live! I live!
Tēnei te tangata pūhuru huru
This is the hairy man
Nāna nei i tiki mai
Who brought the sun
Whakawhiti te rā
And caused it to shine again
Ā upane! Ka upane!
One upward step! Another upward step!
Ā upane, ka upane, whiti te ra!
An upward step, another . . .
the sun shines!
Hi!

WHAT'S IN A NAME?

Where did the names 'New Zealand' and 'Aotearoa' come from?

As far as we know, the Dutch explorer Abel Tasman was the first European to sight New Zealand — the north-west coast of the South Island, to be specific— in 1642. Even though he didn't spend long here, and didn't land, he admired the country and named it Staten Landt, 'In honour of the States General' (Dutch Parliament). On his return to Holland, a cartographer changed the name to Nieuw Zeeland after the Dutch province of Zeeland. It became Nova Zeelandia, from the Latin, and in English then became New Zealand.

In the Māori Declaration of Independence of 1835, which led to the adoption of our first flag (see page 20) by the United Tribes, the country is named (as translated) Nu Tereni, and this, or close versions of the name, was the generally accepted name for the country by early Māori. Even in the Māori translation of the Treaty of Waitangi in 1840, Nu Tirani appears, with no reference to Aotearoa.

So where did Aotearoa come from?

In some modern Māori mythology, when legendary voyager Kupe first saw a line of clouds, he said to his wife Kuramārōtini, also called Hine-te-aparangi, 'Surely that means a point of land' and she exclaimed 'He ao, he ao!' (A cloud, a cloud!) So Kupe named the land Aotea — originally to identify Great Barrier Island (which still keeps this name) and the North Island, and then it became lengthened to Aotearoa, because of the North Island's size. Although the name Aotearoa wasn't originally meant to identify the entire country, it eventually became accepted as the Māori name for New Zealand.

However, there's no evidence that the name was used much at all by Māori, and there's no written record of its use before 1855. There's a 'rebel' flag (left) made by Hēni Te Kirikaramu Pore (Jane Foley) before 1863 which features the word Aotearoa. William Pember Reeves popularised the name and brought it into more general use with both Europeans and Māori when his book entitled *Aotearoa — The Long White Cloud* was published in 1898.

In 2013, the names of our three main islands were officially designated in Māori as Te Ika-a-Māui (the fish of Māui) for the North Island, Te Waipounamu (the waters of greenstone) for the South Island, and Rakiura (glowing skies) for Stewart Island.

In the legends of the Māori folk hero Māui, the South Island is his waka, Stewart Island is its anchor stone, and the North Island is the great fish that he caught — its mouth is Wellington, Northland is its tail, and the fins are the East Coast and Taranaki. Lake Taupō is the fish's heart, and Lake Wairarapa is one of its eyes. Other traditions have the South Island named as Te Waka a Aoraki (the canoe of Aoraki / Mt Cook and his brothers).

You can find the world's longest place name — 85 letters long — at Porangahau, in Hawke's Bay. The name is Taumatawhakatangihangakoauauotamateaturipukakapi-kimaungahoronukupokaiwhenuakitanatahu, which means: The brow of the hill where Tamatea, the man with the big knees who slid, climbed and swallowed mountains, known as Traveller, played on his flute to his loved one.

There are other versions of the name which are even longer, up to 92 letters — but just 'Taumata' will often suffice if you need to ask directions.

Even though Māori had established perfectly good place names throughout most of the country, many early Europeans decided to re-name quite a few of them.

For example, Kirikiriroa — a long stretch of gravel — was renamed Hamilton. Tāmaki Makaurau — isthmus of a thousand lovers became Auckland. Ōtepoti — the place of the corners — became Dunedin. Papaoiea — how beautiful it is — was once the name for the location of Palmerston North, and one suburb still keeps that name. The original name for Marton was Tutaenui, which means big dung heap.

Translated, Mount Maunganui actually means mount big mountain. And Mount Taranaki could translate to mount bare mount.

Māori — The word just means something normal or usual. Māori tangata, for example, just means 'an ordinary man'.
Pākehā — The word came into being in the late 1700s, to identify the newly arrived fair-skinned Europeans — essentially it just means people other than Māori. The origin might be from pakepakehā or patupaiarehe (mythical beings resembling men).

'GOD DEFEND NEW ZEALAND'

Our national anthem first began as a poem written by Thomas Bracken of Dunedin in the 1870s. In 1876 a competition was held (with a prize of ten guineas — over $1000 today) to find suitable music for it. The winner was John J. Woods of Otago, and the song was first performed on Christmas Day, 1876, at the Queens Theatre in Dunedin.

The Māori version was written in 1878 by Thomas H. Smith, of Auckland.

Over time, it came to be regarded as our national song or hymn, as 'God Save the Queen' was our national anthem. Although it was played at ceremonies such as the Olympic Games, it was not until 1977 that 'God Defend New Zealand' was given equal national anthem status with 'God Save the Queen'. The first verse of 'God Defend New Zealand' is usually sung in Māori first, followed by the English translation.

E Ihowā Atua,
Oh Lord, God
O ngā iwi mātou rā,
Of nations and of us too
Āta whakarongona;
Listen to us
Me aroha noa
Cherish us

Kia hua ko te pai;
Let goodness flourish
Kia tau tō atawhai;
May your blessings flow
Manaakitia mai
Defend
Aotearoa
New Zealand

God of nations at Thy feet,
In the bonds of love we meet,
Hear our voices, we entreat,
God defend our free land.
Guard Pacific's triple star
From the shafts of strife
and war,
Make her praises heard afar,
God defend New Zealand.

And here are the two complete versions

God of nations at Thy feet,
In the bonds of love we meet,
Hear our voices, we entreat,
God defend our free land.
Guard Pacific's triple star
From the shafts of strife and war,
Make her praises heard afar,
God defend New Zealand.

Men of every creed and race,
Gather here before Thy face,
Asking Thee to bless this place,
God defend our free land.
From dissension, envy, hate,
And corruption guard our state,
Make our country good and great,
God defend New Zealand.

Peace, not war, shall be our boast,
But, should foes assail our coast,
Make us then a mighty host,
God defend our free land.
Lord of battles in Thy might,
Put our enemies to flight,
Let our cause be just and right,
God defend New Zealand.

Let our love for Thee increase,
May Thy blessings never cease,
Give us plenty, give us peace,
God defend our free land.
From dishonour and from shame,
Guard our country's spotless name,
Crown her with immortal fame,
God defend New Zealand.

May our mountains ever be
Freedom's ramparts on the sea,
Make us faithful unto Thee,
God defend our free land.
Guide her in the nations' van,
Preaching love and truth to man,
Working out Thy glorious plan,
God defend New Zealand.

E Ihowā Atua,
O ngā iwi mātou rā,
Āta whakarāngona;
Me aroha noa
Kia hua ko te pai;
Kia tau tō atawhai;
Manaakitia mai
Aotearoa

Waiho tona takiwā
Ko te ao mārama;
Kia whiti tōna rā
Taiāwhio noa.
Ko te hae me te ngangau
Meinga kia kore kau;
Waiho i te rongo mau
Aotearoa

Ōna mano tāngata
Kiri whero, kiri mā,
Iwi Māori, Pākehā,
Rūpeke katoa,
Nei ka tono ko ngā hē
Māu e whakaahu kē,
Kia ora mārire
Aotearoa

Tōna pai me toitū
Tika rawa, pono pū;
Tōna noho, tāna tū;
Iwi nō Ihowā.
Kaua mōna whakamā;
Kia hau te ingoa;
Kia tū hei tauira;
Aotearoa

Tōna mana kia tū!
Tōna kaha kia ū;
Tōna rongo hei pakū
Ki te ao katoa
Aua rawa ngā whawhai
Ngā tutū e tata mai;
Kia tupu nui ai
Aotearoa

Thomas Bracken also came up with the term 'God's Own Country' in another of his poems, and we still use it today — though we've shortened it now to simply Godzone.

At the medal ceremony for the New Zealand rowing eight's victory at the Munich Olympics in 1972, 'God Defend New Zealand' was played as the flags were raised — the first time it was used at an international event.

OUR GOVERNMENT

New Zealand is formally described as a unitary parliamentary constitutional monarchy — we are a member of the British Commonwealth of Nations, with the British monarch as our head of state.

While New Zealand was a colony of Great Britain, it was administered by colonial secretaries and then premiers — a term which was used until 1899. After becoming a dominion within the British Empire in 1907 — a sort of step up in status — we became self-governing.

Every three years we have a general election; we vote for people in our electorates to represent us in parliament, and we have a second vote for whichever political party we prefer, for a total of 120 members of parliament. The political party — or parties — that receive the most votes form a government (with a prime minister at its head), which stays in power until the next election.

Prime Ministers and their Political Parties

1893–1906 Richard Seddon (Liberal)
1906 William Hall-Jones (Liberal)
1906–1912 Joseph Ward (Liberal)
1912 Thomas Mackenzie (Liberal)
1912–1925 William Massey (Reform)
1925 Francis Bell (Reform)
1925–1928 Gordon Coates (Reform)
1930–1935 George Forbes (United)
1935–1940 Michael Joseph Savage (Labour)
1940–1949 Peter Fraser (Labour)
1949–1957 Sidney Holland (National)
1957 Keith Holyoake (National)
1957–1960 Walter Nash (Labour)
1960–1972 Keith Holyoake (National)
1972 Jack Marshall (National)
1972–1974 Norman Kirk (Labour)
1974 Hugh Watt (Labour)
1974–1975 Bill Rowling (Labour)
1975–1984 Robert Muldoon (National)
1984–1989 David Lange (Labour)
1989–1990 Geoffrey Palmer (Labour)
1990 Mike Moore (Labour)
1990–1997 Jim Bolger (National)
1997–1999 Jenny Shipley (National)
1999–2008 Helen Clark (Labour)
2008–2016 John Key (National)
2016–2017 Bill English (National)
2017–2023 Jacinda Ardern (Labour)
2023– Chris Hipkins (Labour)

Governors-General

Since 1841, a governor or governor-general has represented the British Crown in New Zealand.

As Governor

1841–1842 William Hobson
1843–1845 Robert Fitzroy
1845–1853 George Grey
1855–1861 Thomas Gore Brown
1861–1868 George Grey
1868–1873 George Ferguson Bowen
1873–1874 James Fergusson
1875–1879 George Phipps
1879–1880 Hercules Robinson
1880–1882 Arthur Hamilton-Gordon
1883–1889 William Jervois
1889–1892 William Onslow
1892–1897 David Boyle
1897–1904 Uchter Knox
1904–1910 William Plunket
1910–1912 John Dickson-Poynder
1912–1917 Arthur Foljambe

As Governor-General

1917–1920 Arthur Foljambe
1920–1924 John Jellicoe
1924–1930 Charles Fergusson
1930–1935 Charles Bathurst
1935–1941 George Monckton-Arundell
1941–1946 Cyril Newall
1946–1952 Bernard Freyberg
1952–1957 Willoughby Norrie
1957–1962 Charles Lyttelton
1962–1967 Bernard Fergusson
1967–1972 Arthur Porritt
1972–1977 Denis Blundell
1977–1980 Keith Holyoake
1980–1985 David Beattie
1985–1990 Paul Reeves
1990–1996 Catherine Tizard
1996–2001 Michael Hardie Boys
2001–2006 Silvia Cartwright
2006–2011 Anand Satyanand
2011–2016 Jerry Mateparae
2016–2021 Patsy Reddy
2021– Cindy Kiro

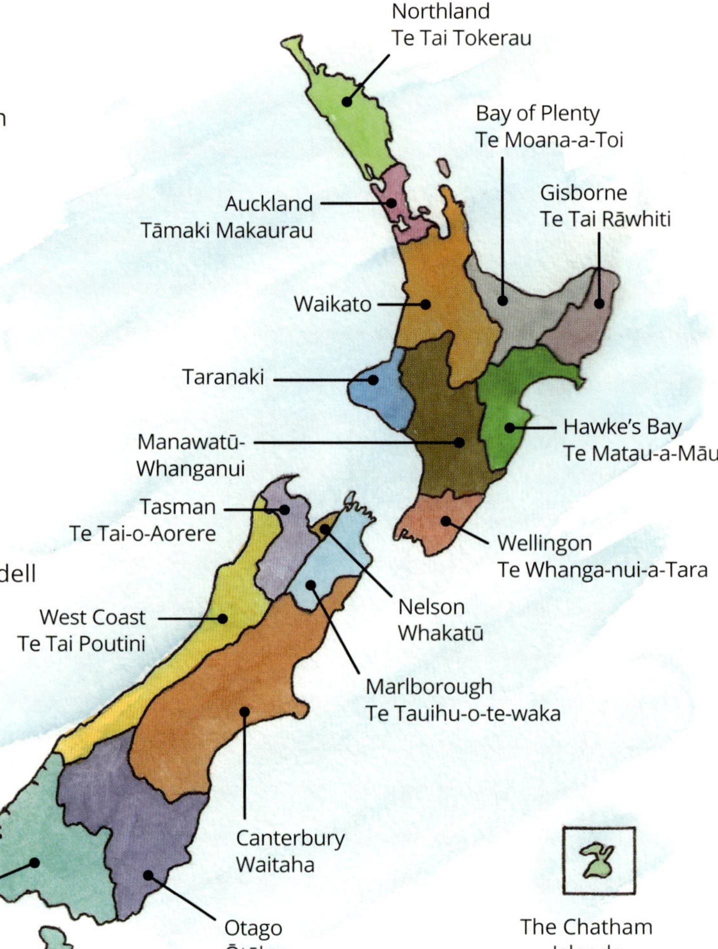

OUR COAT OF ARMS

The use of the official New Zealand coat of arms is very restricted. Generally, it can only be used by government departments. It appears on the flag of our governor-general, and on a flag flown when the British monarch is in New Zealand. On special occasions, permission to use it may be given.

The first quarter of the shield shows four stars that represent the Southern Cross, then three ships symbolising the importance of New Zealand's sea trade. In the second quarter a fleece represents the farming industry. The wheat sheaf in the third quarter represents the agricultural industry, and the crossed hammers in the fourth quarter represent mining.

The supporters on either side of the shield are a European woman holding the New Zealand flag and a Māori rangatira holding a taiaha. St Edward's Crown, shown above the shield, is used in the coronation of the monarch. The crown symbolises the British monarch as the monarch of New Zealand under the New Zealand Royal Titles Act 1953.

A design competition was held in 1906 and 1908 to establish a coat of arms for New Zealand. Seventy-five entries were received, which included Union Jacks, Māori warriors, stars, ships, and also kiwi, moa, sheep, cows . . . and even lions!

The best three were sent to London for final judging, and the winner was an entry from James McDonald, a draughtsman in the Department of Tourist and Health Resorts. A royal warrant granting the design was issued in 1911. The description of the arms lead to many interpretations, and at least 20 different versions were found to be in use in the mid-1940s.

A design committee then redrew and standardised the coat of arms — tweaking a few elements of the 1911 original, for example, the two supporters were looking away from each other in the first design — and this revised version was then approved by Queen Elizabeth II in 1956.

WHICH FLAG?

As ships began trading from New Zealand, they carried no official flag, which meant they could be subject to seizure or confiscation from other nations. To counter this and to protect our shipping, a flag was chosen in 1834 by a gathering of 25 Northland rangatira, or chiefs, to be flown on New Zealand vessels. This is the flag of the United Tribes of New Zealand (right).

In 1840 the Treaty of Waitangi was signed, and we became a British colony; and while the Union Jack replaced the United Tribes flag, we then gained a new flag for our shipping — the British Blue Ensign, with the letters NZ at lower right.

Many Māori believed that the United Tribes should be flown alongside the Union Jack, to represent their equal status, and Ngāpuhi chief Hōne Heke famously felled the flagstaff at Kororāreka several times in protest.

The next change was to the flag we use today (left). First Lieutenant Albert Markham of HMS *Blanche* suggested a new design to the Governor of New Zealand, George Bowen, and it was adopted for use on ships in 1869, and then became our national flag in 1902. Again based on the British Blue Ensign, with the Union Jack in the top left corner, it carries the stars of the Southern Cross in red, and outlined in white.

Our other national flag — although unofficial — is the silver fern on a black background (above). Famously used by the All Blacks, it's also an image used by many businesses, sporting bodies, on military uniforms and vehicles — even by our national airline, Air New Zealand, and it's known all around the world as an identifier of Kiwis and New Zealand.

There have been many suggestions for a new flag over the years.

Austrian artist Friedensreich Hundertwasser designed the green koru flag (below), derived from the natural koru curve. By the way, Hundertwasser also designed the eccentric public toilets in Kawakawa.

A referendum (full national vote) to find a new flag — or keep the current one — was held in 2015 and also in 2016. These were some of the contenders:

The Tino Rangatiratanga flag (right) was designed by Hiraina Marsden, Jan Smith and Linda Munn in 1990, and is now often used by Māori. After a nationwide iwi vote in 2010 it was adopted as the national Māori flag, although many Māori still preferred the original United Tribes flag.

Kyle Lockwood's Silver Fern (above) was the flag chosen in the second referendum to compete with the current flag — a direct choice between two flags. It keeps the colours of the current flag, and incorporates the silver fern, the Southern Cross and the deep blue background. It failed to win voters' hearts, though . . . the existing flag was retained with a 57 per cent vote.

Andrew Fyfe's Koru (above) — with a dramatic black-and-white nod to Hundertwasser's effort — represents 'new life, growth and peace'.

Influenced by Māori taniko weaving patterns, Aaron Dustin's Red Peak (right) is one of the boldest designs. It represents 'land, light and position'.

Michael Smythe's Walters Koru (above) is inspired by the work of Gordon Walters. Using the koru, it displays the union of the two principal races in New Zealand — Pākehā and Māori.

NEW ZEALAND – SMALL OR BIG?

It depends how you look at it. If you're looking at a map of the world, then New Zealand does look rather small. However, that could just be because we are such a long way from everyone else, so it's hard to compare. (We're about 1500 kilometres from Australia, just over 3,000 kilometres from Antarctica and 10,400 kilometres from the United States.)

New Zealand is 268,021 square kilometres in size, and it would take 36 New Zealands to equal the size of the United States (9,834,000 square kilometres) . . . and if we were a US state, we would rank as the ninth largest! And compared to Russia — well, it would take 63 New Zealands to equal that massive country's 17,130,000 square kilometres!

Of 199 sovereign nations in the world, we rank 73rd in size, behind Burkina Faso (it's in Africa, in case you didn't know!) at 273,600 square kilometres, and ahead of Gabon (also Africa) at 257,670 square kilometres.

New Zealand was the last of the world's major landmasses to be 'discovered' by European explorers (of course, voyaging Polynesians had discovered and settled these islands hundreds of years previously) and for another 200 years or so our remoteness meant that getting here was quite a major undertaking: even travelling from Australia — our closest neighbour — could take several days by ship.

In 1891, writer and poet Rudyard Kipling said of us *Last, loneliest, loveliest, exquisite, apart* — well, he said it about Tāmaki Makaurau or Auckland actually, but it applies to the whole country, too.

But on the other hand, we're quite large!

We're larger than Great Britain by nearly 59,000 square kilometres, and considerably larger than some other European countries . . . we're larger than eight Belgiums, or six Netherlands or Denmarks, for example.

New Zealand is also the seventh-largest island nation in the world, and the third largest in the Southern Hemisphere.

Before some recent reclamation work, the state of Singapore could've fitted into Lake Taupō's 616 square kilometres (though it's just a little bit too big for that now; see page 29) . . . and the island of Niue (261 square kilometres) could fit into Lake Taupō twice with plenty of room to spare!

New Zealand is 1600 kilometres in length, and 400 kilometres wide at the widest point. Our coastline is over 18,000 kilometres in length — if it was possible to walk around the coast non-stop at an average walking speed of 3.5 kilometres per hour, it would take about 5142 hours to get back to the start . . . that's over seven and a half months! Tiring!

New Zealand has well over 600 islands, and about 150 of them can be found in the Bay of Islands.

In square kilometres, the largest are . . .

1. South Island — 150,437 (because it's the biggest, South Islanders reckon it's the nation's mainland!)
2. North Island — 113,729
3. Stewart Island/Rakiura — 1746
4. Chatham Island — 920
5. Auckland Island (Southern Pacific) — 510
6. Great Barrier Island/Aotea (Hauraki Gulf) — 285
7. Resolution Island (Fiordland) — 208
8. D'Urville Island (Marlborough Sounds) — 150
9. Campbell Island (Southern Pacific) — 115
10. Adams Island (Southern Pacific) — 100
11. Waiheke Island (Hauraki Gulf) — 92

WHY DO WE HAVE EARTHQUAKES?

It's all to do with the tectonic plates that make up the Earth's crust. There are about eight very large plates — much larger than continents — and many small ones. They can range from 6 kilometres in thickness up to 40 kilometres, and rest on deep layers of hot molten rock. These underlying layers are moving in very slow motion all the time, and push and pull the plates above. Movement of the plates around the world usually varies from 0–100 millimetres each year.

Plates may push directly into each other, and one may slowly dominate and rise over the other, forcing it beneath . . . over great periods of time this creates higher land and eventually mountain ranges. Other plates might be stable and essentially unmoving, or slowly passing each other without any great friction. And some are even moving apart, to create rifts and valleys, especially in the deep oceans.

Plates often get pushed in different directions, which can cause them to grind against each other and sometimes lock up. In these situations, pressure increases until the plates find and force a way past, which creates tremors, shaking and reverberations in the ground — it's an earthquake!

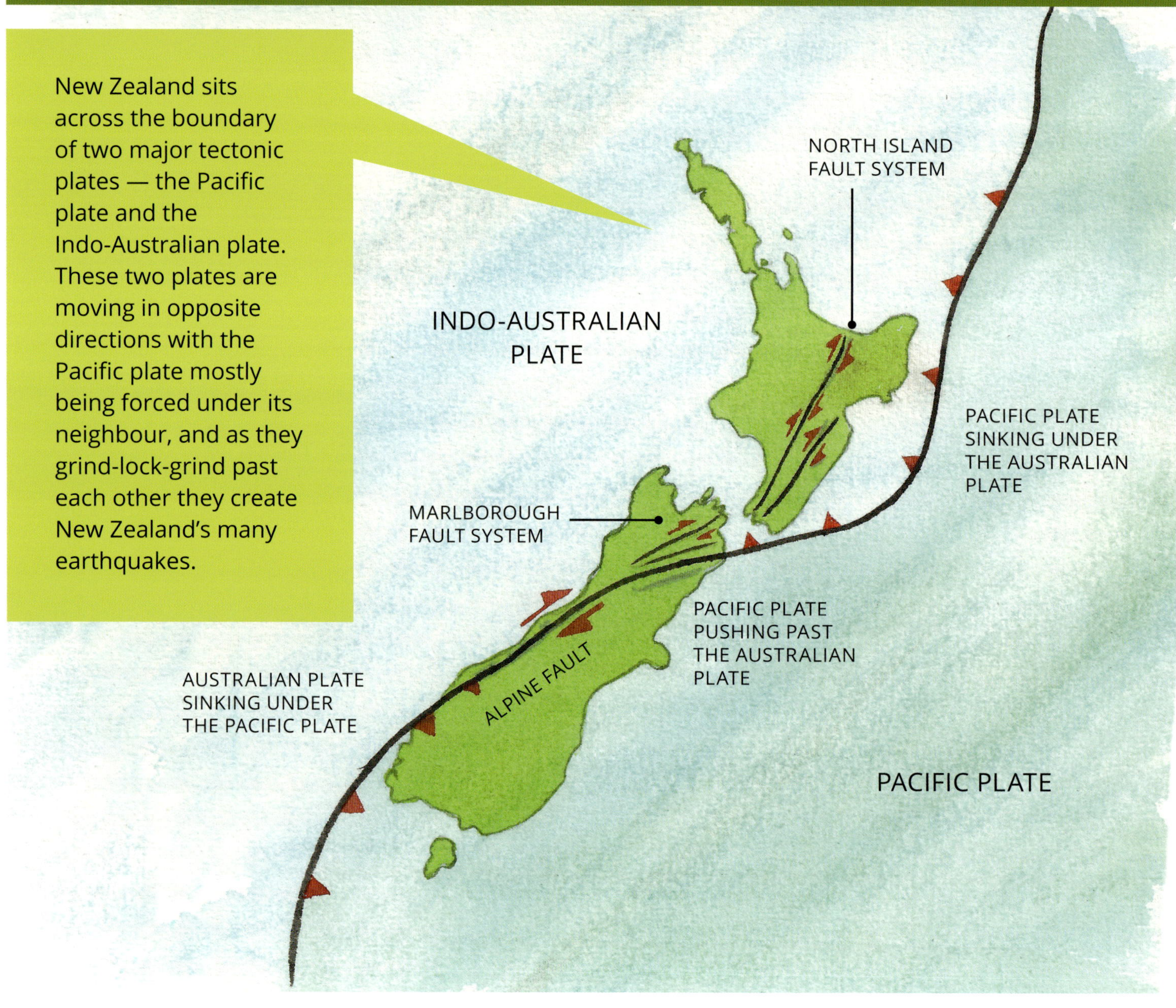

New Zealand experiences over 15,000 earthquakes each year, although most are light enough to register only on seismographs — machines that can detect even the most 'delicate' tremors in the ground. Only about 100–150 are actually felt by us.

Quakes are measured by magnitude. On average, we can expect several quakes at magnitude 6 each year, one magnitude 7 every decade, and a magnitude 8 every century.

The push-and-pull effect of the two tectonic plates through our country means that the North Island is getting stretched by about 8 millimetres each year. The shape of New Zealand has continually been affected by the motion of the two plates — basically, the Australian plate is moving northwards, while the Pacific plate heads west. This conflict forced land to rise, creating the South Island's Southern Alps, and produced fault lines and weaknesses through the country — the North Island's 'hot spots' for example (see next pages).

In 1769, Captain Cook documented the first official report of a New Zealand earthquake, and from that point on, we've increasingly been nicknamed 'The Shaky Isles'.

While there have been devasting earthquakes in relatively recent times, such as Napier in 1931, Christchurch 2010–2011 and Kaikoura 2016 — all with loss of lives and tremendous damage to buildings — the most powerful earthquake to hit Aotearoa was the magnitude 8.2 Wairarapa/Wellington earthquake of 1855. Some 5,000 square kilometres of land was uplifted — land at Turakirae Head rose by over 6 metres, and great stretches of new shoreline were exposed. The unlocking of the tectonic plates along the fault line caused a horizontal movement of around 18 metres — the greatest shift ever recorded, and twice that of the catastrophic San Francisco earthquake of 1906.

VOLCANOES

New Zealand has a lot of volcanic activity, due to the slow grinding collision of the two tectonic plates on which the country sits (see previous pages). This creates faults and weaknesses in the ground, which allows hot magma (molten rock) to push up to the surface. Sometimes the pressure from below can be so great that the magma bursts up and out in a volcanic eruption of molten rock and poisonous gasses . . . which can cause destruction and loss of life.

Most of our volcanic activity is through the centre of the North Island, and extends far out through the ocean to Raoul Island — hundreds of kilometres to the north-east.

Our most active volcanoes are Ruapehu and Ngāuruhoe — Ruapehu has erupted 18 times in the last 1800 years, while Ngāuruhoe has erupted about 60 times since 1839.

Ruapehu translates as pit of noise or exploding pit, while Ngāuruhoe translates as throwing hot stones.

Whakaari/White Island in the Bay of Plenty is one of our hottest and more dangerous volcanoes — some of its rocks and gasses can reach temperatures of 250 degrees Celsius! Its venting of poisonous gasses has caused tragic worker and visitor deaths in 1914 and 2019.

It's estimated that one in 20 people all around the world live within what's called the danger range of an active volcano, resulting in about 540 deaths annually. Volcanic activity accounts for about 1.5 billion dollars of property damage and loss each year.

Auckland sits on a massive volcanic field that has seen over 50 eruptions from individual volcanoes in the last 250,000 years. The youngest of them all is Rangitoto, which rose from the sea about 600 years ago. Its name means sky blood after its undoubtedly spectacular eruption display was witnessed by local Māori.

New Zealand's greatest volcanic eruptions created Lake Taupō. That particular hot spot has erupted many times, with the most devastating eruptions occuring about 30,000 years ago, and another nearly 2000 years ago. Both times a huge mass of rocks, ash and gas — several kilometres high — was ejected, and then collapsed and poured out across the North Island at rates faster than the speed of sound. Most of it swept eastwards and completely destroyed the lush forests around Taupō, leaving the land devastated. If that immense mass of material could be evenly distributed, it would likely cover all of New Zealand to a depth of 45 metres.

This gigantic blast created Lake Taupō; the lake is simply the sunken mouth — the caldera — of the dead volcano. The magma chamber now lies about 6–8 kilometres below the lake.

We see the effects of the heat under our feet in different ways. When underground water becomes heated it can burst through the faults and fissures in the rock. The general area around Rotorua and Taupō has countless vents of hot water and scalding mud pools. Before bores were driven in large numbers to repurpose the steam and water for washing, bathing and cooking, which reduced the overall underground pressure, there were many super geysers which attracted visitors to the area. The giant of them all — and by far the most powerful the world has ever seen — was the Waimangu geyser, which (between 1900 and 1908) could vent a towering column of scalding water and material to great heights (see page 37).

There are several hot-water springs around the North Island, where visitors can enjoy a warm soak in the bubbling, sulphur/eggy-smelling waters. There's even a Hot Water Beach on the Coromandel Peninsula where visitors can dig down into the sand and create their own personal hot spa!

MOUNTAINS, PEAKS AND HILLS

New Zealand has plenty of mountains, and the South Island has most of them — with more than 200 peaks over 2300 metres in height, while the North Island has just two peaks of that size. The South Island is getting higher, as well; the movement of continental plates (see page 24) is pushing it upwards a few millimetres each year!

Here's a selection of the heights of some of our more significant peaks:

1st. 3724 m — Aoraki/Mt Cook (it used to be much taller — an avalanche in 1991 caused it to lose about 20 metres. Doesn't sound like much, but that's about 14 million cubic metres of rock and ice!). About 80 people have died attempting to climb this mountain.

2nd. 3497 m — Mt Tasman

3rd. 3440 m — Mt Dampier

9th. 3033 m — Mt Aspiring

19th. 2979 m — Mt Ruapehu (the highest North Island peak)

65th. 2518 m — Mt Taranaki (sees more climbers per year — about 20,000 — than all 'true' mountains)

116th. 2287 m — Mt Ngāuruhoe

136th. 1978 m — Mt Tongariro

155th. 1683 m — Mitre Peak

183rd. 1111 m — Mt Tarawera

333rd. 399 m — Te Mata Peak, Hastings

339th. 299 m — Brooklyn Hill, Wellington

343rd. 260 m — Rangitoto Island, Hauraki Gulf

344th. 232 m — Mt Maunganui (it would take more than 16 Mt Maunganuis stacked on top of each other to equal Mt Cook!)

347th. 182 m — Maungakiekie/One Tree Hill, Auckland

And this is how they compare in a standard shape — as pyramids! And by the way — the Great Pyramid of Giza, in Egypt, is just 137 metres in height.

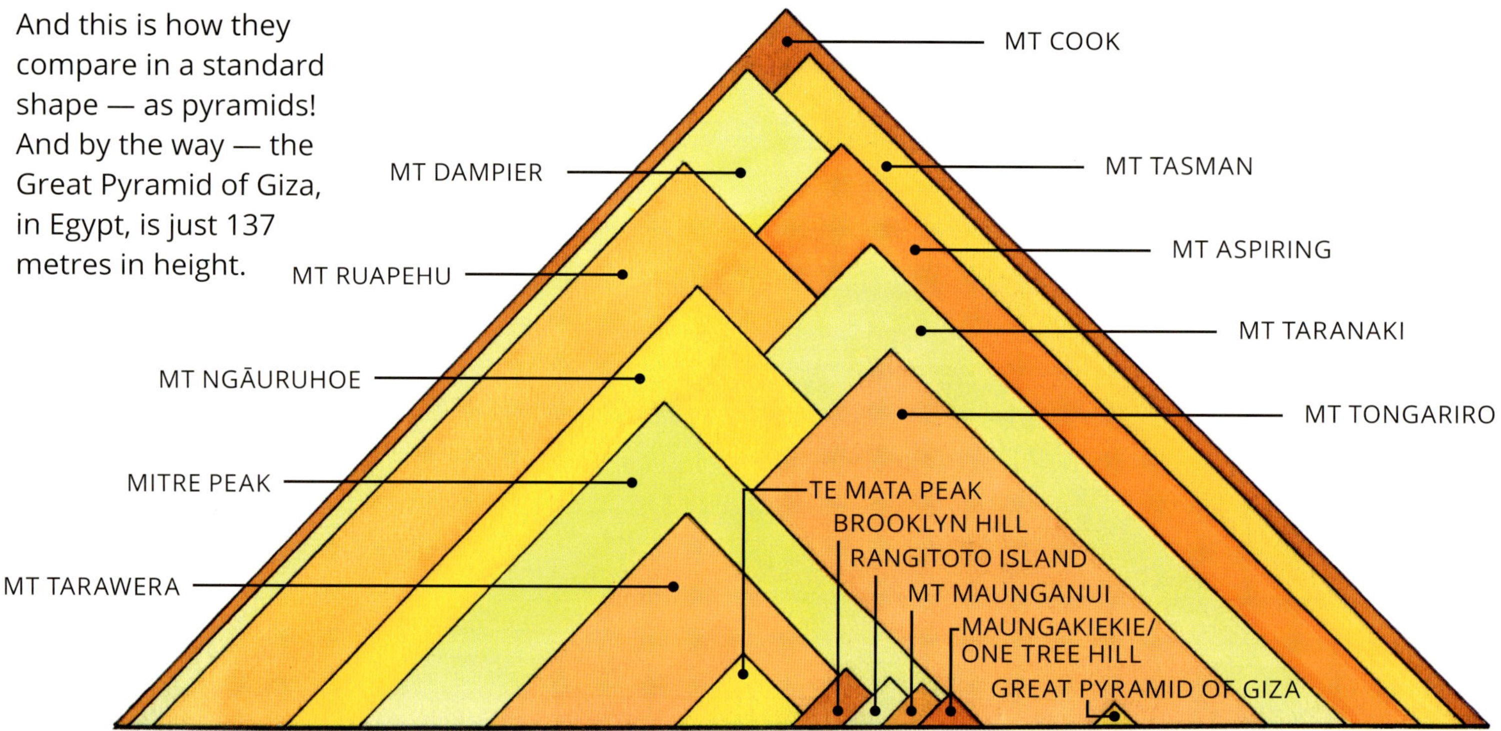

The average height above sea level of the North Island is 298 metres, and the average height above sea level of the South Island is 627 metres. If you take out the extremes of the highest mountains, about three-quarters of the country is actually at an average of 200 metres above sea level. The lowest point in New Zealand is on the Taieri Plain, south of Dunedin, which is 2 metres below sea level.

WHAT A LOT OF WATER!

There are about 800 lakes around the country, and the largest is Lake Taupō at 623 square kilometres (159 metres deep) — which is almost the size of all of Singapore!

The second largest is Lake Te Anau at 344 square kilometres (276 metres deep). Lake Wakatipu is third at 293 square kilometres (378 metres deep). Wakatipu is also our longest lake, at 77 kilometres.

Fiordland's Lake Hauroko is our deepest lake, at 462 metres — it could swallow the Auckland Sky Tower, with room to spare!

Christchurch's Lake Ellesmere is the shallowest — at just 2 metres in depth, even though its area is 182 square kilometres.

The most powerful river is the Buller River (177 kilometres long). In the 1920s a flood flow of 10,400 cubic metres of water per second was estimated — that's nearly 250 olympic-sized swimming pools of water rushing past every minute!

Chatham Island's Te Whanga Lagoon is more than twice the size of Wellington Harbour.

If all the major streams and rivers in the country could be laid end to end, they'd measure about 425,000 kilometres in length — enough to go around the world ten times!

Our longest river — at 425 kilometres — is the Waikato.

Next longest is the Clutha at 322 kilometres. Third is the Whanganui at 290 kilometres. There are seven more rivers over 200 kilometres in length; another 26 over 100 kilometres long; and another 20 more than 50 kilometres long.

Our shortest recognised river is the Turanganui River at Gisborne — it's just 0.9 kilometre long.

At 0° Centigrade, water freezes and becomes ice — and we've got plenty of that. The South Island has about 3,155 glaciers larger than 2.5 acres (that's more than a dozen suburban sections). Mount Ruapehu in the North Island has about 18 small glaciers — one even sits within the crater. New Zealand's largest — at 23.5 kilometres in length — is the Haupapa/ Tasman Glacier in the Aoraki/Mt Cook area in the Southern Alps. Its ice is 600 metres deep in places and covers an area of over 100 square kilometres.

Close by are the Murchison Glacier (18 kilometres long), and the Fox (13 kilometres) and Franz Josef (12 kilometres) glaciers.

In New Zealand's ice ages, many thousands of years ago, the weight and force of giant glaciers cut and created deep mountain valleys. As the ice slowly retreated from the valleys near the coast, the sea came in to form the deep fiords we have today.

Fiordland has 14 true fiords — the largest are Dusky Sound (44 kilometres long) Doubtful Sound (40 kilometres) and Preservation Inlet (36 kilometres).

It's believed that our glaciers held about 73 billion tonnes of ice in 1949. With atmospheric temperatures rising since that time, it's now down to less than half that figure.

From 1997 to 2016, over 15 cubic kilometres of ice was lost from our glaciers — that's enough to fill Wellington Harbour 12 times!

If all the ice from our glaciers could be made into a single giant ice cube, it would contain about 40 cubic kilometres of ice (that's somewhere in the region of 120 trillion tonnes) and measure 3.5 kilometres on each side — and stand nearly as tall as Mt Cook!

There are different claims about which is the highest waterfall in Aotearoa. Some claim Sutherland Falls (near Milford Sound) is the highest, which drops a total of 580 metres in three stages. Browne Falls in Doubtful Sound is higher at about 826 metres, but the water might be regarded as a cascade rather a clean drop, as it doesn't freefall through the air. If Browne Falls is recognised as the highest in New Zealand, it would be the 12th highest in the world.

Meanwhile, the nearby Terror Falls (740 metres) and Chamberlain Falls (700 metres) can safely claim impressive third and fourth places.

The most powerful is the Huka Falls, near Taupō. At this point, the normally calm waters of the Waikato River are forced into a rocky narrow ravine and over the 11-metre drop. The result is a thundering torrent of up to 270 cubic metres of water per second through the narrow gap — roughly equal to a million garden hoses going full blast!

New Zealand can boast of one the most powerful natural springs in the world. Te Waikoropupū Springs, near Tākaka in the South Island, are our largest freshwater springs, and the greatest cold-water springs in the Southern Hemisphere. They're one of the most powerful springs in the world, with an average flow of 14 cubic metres per second. They also boast some of the cleanest water ever tested.

So where does all this water come from? Rain! New Zealand gets plenty of it. The average yearly rainfall throughout the country can be anywhere between 640 and 1500 millimetres. Milford Sound is the wettest single locality in New Zealand, with an average yearly rainfall of nearly 7000 millimetres — it rains there about 180 days each year. The South Island's West Coast sees the greatest average yearly rainfall of all the country's regions; usually somewhere between 2000 and 10,000 millimetres. The greatest deluge recorded was in Tauranga in 1948, when 34 millimetres of rain fell in just one 10-minute period. The greatest rainfall in a single day — 758 millimetres — was at the Cropp River, near Hokitika, in 1989. The longest period without rain was at Wai-iti, in Marlborough, in 1939 — which saw 71 days without a single drop! It's no surprise that Wai-iti means little water.

NATURAL TREASURES AND ICONS

Most people would probably agree that our most precious natural treasure, or taonga, is greenstone — pounamu. It holds a very special place in traditional Māori culture. It was once used to make the blades of tools, such as knives, adzes and chisels, for making weapons like mere (hand clubs) and spear points, and items of jewellery, such as hei tiki, pendants and combs.

Pounamu is found only in the South Island, and in 1997 Ngāi Tahu — the principal iwi of the South Island — was officially reinstated by the Crown as the official owner of all naturally occurring pounamu, after many years of abuse of the resource by outsiders.

Today anyone is welcome to fossick for pounamu, but mostly at the coast, and only in designated areas, and not for more than can be carried by an individual. Removing pounamu — large river boulders, for example — from protected areas is punishable by law.

Greenstone comes in several forms of closely-related stone — nephrite jade, bowenite and serpentinite, and in a range of shades, colourings and markings.

Greenstone boulder

Modern pendant

Hei tiki

In Māori culture it is frowned upon to buy pounamu for oneself — it has no special meaning. It's much better and more significant to receive it as a gift.

Although related species can be found around the Pacific region, it's only in New Zealand that kauri grow to such tremendous sizes. For Māori, kauri was second only to totara for use in constructing the great waka taua — war canoes. Early Europeans appreciated its worth too, and logged great areas of forest for timber in general construction and ship-building. Even the trees' sap was greedily sought — for a while in the late 1800s the value of exports of kauri gum well exceeded that of gold!

Today, the remaining kauri forests — in Northland — are properly protected. The largest kauri is the 2000-year-old Tane Mahuta, in the Waipoua Forest, with a total height of over 50 metres. The largest kauri ever officially measured was Kairaru, which was twice the size, and twice the age, of Tane Mahuta. Kairaru was destroyed by fire in the 1800s.

Kowhaiwhai

Fern koru

Another treasure from plants is the simple koru — the uncurling spiral of a young fern frond. It's an important emblem of Māori art and culture, and appears in many carvings, paintings and in the decoration of weapons, jewellery and waka. It can be simple or complex as in the kowhaiwhai paintings in the rafters of marae buildings. Many organisations, companies and artists have embraced and employed the shape over the years. The word koru simply means loop.

There's no bird in the world like the kiwi. An extra-long bill, with nostrils at the end (all the better for sniffing and snuffling out small prey from the undergrowth). No proper wings to speak of (apart from tiny ones under all those coarse feathers, just big enough for the bird to tuck in its bill, when curling up to sleep). It has whiskers like a cat, and it lays the largest egg (comparative to body size) of any bird in the world — and brown kiwi sometimes lay two! And it lives in holes in the ground! It's a remarkable bird, and the image of the kiwi has been used as our national symbol, and in products and advertising, since the first days of European settlement. It's no wonder that we're known to the rest of the world as simply Kiwis.

The tuatara is certainly one of our natural treasures. It's been around — practically unchanged — since the early days of the dinosaurs. There are two species and, as a result of the damage caused by introduced predators, both now live mostly on protected islands. There are just four groups of reptiles: alligators and crocodiles; lizards and snakes; turtles and tortoises; and all by itself in the fourth group — the tuatara, found only in Aotearoa.

They can live for a hundred years or more, weigh about a kilogram, and measure more than 60 centimetres from snout to the tip of the tail.

So much of our wildlife can be considered taonga — especially those found nowhere else in the world, or those that need special protection from us in order to survive.

Take the wētā, for example. While there are many wētā species around the world, nowhere else do they reach the impressive size of our giant wētā . . . some as heavy as a blackbird, and nearly the same body size! They might be scary to look at, but they aren't aggressive — they're happy to snack on vegetation, or even the end of a carrot held in your hand! Part of the giant wētā's scientific name is *Deinacrida*, which means terrible grasshopper, and the Māori name — wētāpunga — tranlates as god of ugly things.

Like the tuatara, they made easy prey for introduced predators, and are now mostly restricted to high country or protected islands.

There are many different wētā types in New Zealand besides the giant wētā: tree wētā (the one most commonly encountered by humans); alpine wētā; tusked wētā and cave wētā. Although cave wētā have small bodies — some only 2.5 centimetres in length — they can be a total length of well over 35 centimetres, measured from hind feet to the tips of their extra-long antennae. They're great jumpers, too — they can cover 3 metres in a single bound!

How many animal and plant species are there in New Zealand?

2 tuatara
2 bats
7 frogs
9 seals
20 sea urchins
90 lizards
150 sea stars
200 crabs
200 birds
200 worms
500 sea sponges
600 seaweeds
1000 fish
2500 spiders
3660 shellfish
8500 plants*
20,000 fungi
20,000 insects

*plus another 25,000 introduced plants!

What other treasures are there that need our special attention and care?

Māui's dolphin — our only endemic dolphin (found nowhere else in the world) and the smallest at only 1.5 metres in length. There are just over 50 individuals known.

Kākāpō — just over 200 of these big flightless parrots survive, on protected islands.

Hoiho — the yellow-eyed penguin. One of the world's rarest breeds of penguin (between 4000–5000 individuals), found only around the waters of New Zealand and its sub-Antarctic islands.

Takahē — once thought extinct, but a small population was found in the Murchison Mountains in 1948. Through care, there are now nearly 500 birds surviving, mostly on offshore islands.

NATURAL CURIOSITIES

Caves can be found in all sorts of rock, but limestone rock is home to some of the biggest. The rock gets slowly worn away by water flowing underground for long periods of time, and as the water finds new routes or dries up, caves and passages are left behind. Dripping water from the roofs of these openings contain tiny particles of limestone, which can build up over thousands of years into a hanging (stalactite) or standing (stalagmite) pillar. Sometimes these pillars can meet and form a cave floor-to-ceiling column. There are many caves like this throughout New Zealand, but the Waitomo Caves are famous all around the world for their impressive formations, and for the cave boat trips to see the glow-worms.

In Tākaka Hill there's a great gaping chasm called Harwood's Hole, which is more than deep enough to swallow the Auckland Sky Tower — it has the deepest vertical shaft of any New Zealand cave, at 176 metres — and it's 357 metres to its deepest point!

Another cave capable of 'swallowing' famous buildings is Hollow Hill, near Waitomo. Its cavern is 120,000 cubic metres — more than enough to hide Wellington's Beehive building inside.

The biggest cave systems in New Zealand? There's the Nettlebed at Mount Arthur in the South Island. It's over 24 kilometres long, and 889 metres deep. Nearby is the Ellis Basin cave system — 33.4 kilometres long, and 1024 metres deep — the deepest caves in the Southern Hemisphere. Bulmer Cavern, at Mount Owen in the Tasman District is only 750 metres deep, but its voids and passages run for an impressive 66 kilometres! Curiously, the wee township of Cave, near Timaru, doesn't have any caves at all!

The Putangirua Pinnacles look like transplants from an alien landscape, and the area was used as a location for filming *The Lord of the Rings* for its other-worldly nature.

The pinnacles had their beginnings millions of years ago when the nearby ranges were islands, and loose gravels accumulated along the coast. As waters receded, the gravels were eroded by floods and rain. Some parts — more heavily cemented together — resisted the general erosion and were left as towering misshapen pinnacles, or 'hoodoos'.

The Punakaiki pancake rocks are formed from many layers of plant and animal fragments over tens of millions of years on the seabed, they gradually solidified — kilometres down — under pressure from above, and then were slowly lifted by seismic activity to the surface, where softer layers eroded away to form the stacks of pancakes appearance. There are hollows and shafts inside the formations, where the incoming high-tide seas form great blowholes.

One of our greatest ever natural curiosities was the beautiful Pink and White Terraces, once regarded as one of the natural wonders of the world. The silica-fringed tiered pools — formed by hundreds of years of thermal activity — were destroyed by the eruption of Mt Tarawera in 1886.

The Moeraki Boulders were formed from accumulations of seabed mud over 50 million years ago. The larger boulders would have taken 4–5 million years to grow, while deeply embedded under increasing layers of mud and silt. As land lifted, the softer rocks and soils gradually eroded, and allowed the boulders to become exposed and then roll out onto the shore. Some have reached over 2 metres in diameter and weigh over 7 tonnes. Fossil remains of plesiosaurs and mosasaurs have been found inside large boulders at Shag Point, just south of Moeraki. Even larger spherical boulders — up to 3 metres in diameter — can be seen on the shores of the Hokianga Harbour.

Near Rotorua, the Waimangu geyser — the name means black waters — was once the most powerful geyser in existence, and attracted visitors from around the world. Created partly by the eruption of Mt Tarawera, by 1900 it was regularly erupting black water, rocks and mud from a crater 64 metres across, to a height of 460 metres — far higher than the Auckland Sky Tower (328 metres). In 1903, four visitors were killed when they got too close to the edge of the violent geyser and were swept away. From 1904 its power lessened, and by 1908 it was regarded as extinct.

GOOD SPORTS

Our first individual Olympic medal was won by Harry Kerr, who gained a bronze medal in the 3500-metre walk at the London Olympics in 1908. Our first gold medal was awarded to Malcolm Champion in the 4 x 200-metre freestyle swimming. However, both Kerr and Champion competed in a combined Australia/New Zealand team, called Australasia. In 1920 the first true New Zealand team — just four competitors — competed at the Antwerp Olympics, and Darcy Hadfield claimed a bronze medal in rowing. In 1924 Arthur Porritt took bronze in the 100 metres in Paris, and Ted Morgan took our first New Zealand gold medal in boxing. One of our most famous track victories came when Jack Lovelock took gold in the thrilling finish of the 1500 metres at the 1936 Berlin Olympics. Previously, he'd broken the English mile record in 1933, set a new world mile record in 1933, and won gold in the mile event at the British Empire Games in 1934.

As of 2022, New Zealand has won a total of 140 Olympic medals — 53 gold, 34 silver and 53 bronze. Our best Olympic Games was at Tokyo in 2021, winning a total of 20 medals.

In the Commonwealth Games we've won a total of 657 medals — 159 gold, 220 silver and 278 bronze. And we mustn't forget the Winter Olympics, where we've won a total of six medals.

Bob Fitzsimmons was just 10 years old when his family came here from England in 1873. Just seven years later he entered a boxing tournament in Timaru, and knocked out all four of his opponents in one night! He later turned professional, and after some fights in the USA, he challenged the famous Jack Dempsey for the World Middleweight Championship in 1891, and knocked Dempsey out in the 13th round. He defended his title in 1894 by knocking out Dan Creedon (another New Zealander) in the second round. In 1897 he beat James J. Corbett to become the World Heavyweight Champion — knocking him out in the 14th round. He lost the title at the first defence, but then went on to claim the World Light-Heavyweight Championship in 1905, and became the first boxer to win world championships at three different weights.

In 1880, 'Torpedo Billy' Murphy, from Auckland, knocked out Irishman Ike Weir in San Francisco to claim the world featherweight boxing title. And it was to be another 136 years before a New Zealand-born boxer — heavyweight Joseph Parker — claimed a world boxing title.

Anthony Wilding of Christchurch was our first tennis great and was the world's number one player. In his career, he won 11 grand slam titles — six in singles play, and five in doubles. In 1913, he had a unique triple — winning the World Hard Court Championship, The World Grass Court Championship and the World Covered Court Championship. He was Wimbledon Singles Champion in four successive years — 1910, 1911, 1912 and 1913.

Speedway motorbike rider Ivan Mauger won many world and international titles over his career, and was the Individual Speedway World Champion for a record six times, and runner-up three times. He was voted the Greatest Rider of the 20th Century.

When he won his third world title in 1970, two fans made good on their promise to have his motorbike gold-plated, and it's now part of the collection at Canterbury Museum.

Although New Zealanders have had great success in motor racing around the world — Bruce McLaren and Chris Amon, for example — Denny Hulme, of Motueka, is the only New Zealand driver to have won the Formula One Drivers' Championship — in 1967, while racing for the Brabham team. He raced in 112 grand prix, winning 8 and with 33 appearances on the podium. He appeared in and won races in many other racing disciplines in his career.

Racing car driver Scott Dixon has won the USA's IndyCar Championship six times — in 2003, 2008, 2013, 2015, 2018 and 2020. He also won the Indianapolis 500 in 2008. With his total of 51 wins, he's the third most successful driver in American Championship Cars history.

Runner John Walker was the first person in the world to run a mile under 3:50, and then became the first person to do it 100 times! He also broke the record for the 2000 metres, and the 1500 indoors. He won many races and broke records in New Zealand and around the world, and in 1976 he won gold in the 1500 metres at the Montreal Olympics. He also claimed two silvers and a bronze in the Commonwealth Games.

The most successful New Zealand team of all time has just got to be the All Blacks. New Zealand's national men's rugby union team has been world champions three times, and since world rankings were introduced in 2003, the All Blacks have been rated the number one side for 80 per cent of that time.

From 2000 to 2009, the All Blacks won 100 tests, which was 92% of their total games, and between 2015 and 2016 they had an incredible winning streak of 18 test wins around the world. Between 2009 and 2017 they established the record for the most consecutive test wins played *at home* — 47! They're the only international side to have a winning record against every nation they've played.

ARTS SMART

In 1994, Anna Paquin became the first New Zealander to win an Academy Award (or, as it's also known by its nickname, an Oscar) for her role as Best Supporting Actress in *The Piano*. At just 11 years old, she was the second youngest person ever to receive an Oscar.

First released in 1995, 'How Bizarre' by Pauly Fuemana/OMC was a hit single all around the world, and made it to number one on the USA's Billboard Top 40 in 1997 — the first New Zealand song to do so. It stayed in the USA's Top 40 for 32 weeks.

Peter Jackson's *The Lord of the Rings* trilogy — produced and filmed in New Zealand — was nominated for 30 Oscars, and won 17. The third movie — *The Return of the King* — alone won 11 of these, making it equal with *Ben-Hur* (1959) and *Titanic* (1997) as the highest Oscar-winning movie ever. Box-office ticket sales around the world totalled around US$3 billion for the trilogy.

New Zealander Richard O'Brien's *The Rocky Horror Picture Show* movie was, and still is, a hit all around the world. It began as a musical stage show — *The Rocky Horror Show* — in 1973, and the movie version was released in 1975. It's still being shown around the world, making it the longest-running theatrical release in movie history. A remake — *The Rocky Horror Picture Show: Let's Do the Time Warp Again* — was made for American television in 2016. In 2004, the city of Hamilton erected a statue of O'Brien as Riff Raff — the character he played in the show.

While Josh Nanai (aka Jawsh 685) and Kimbra have topped the UK charts with collaborative hits with other artists, in 2020 and 2012 respectively, Lorde was the first to achieve it as a solo artist in 2013 with her song 'Royals'. The song was a number one hit all around the world — selling more than 10,000,000 units — and stayed at the top of the USA's Billboard Hot 100 for nine weeks.

Len Lye (1901–1980) was one of New Zealand's most significant artists, who worked in experimental movies (marking directly onto film stock) and kinetic (moving) sculptures. While many of his works are in prestigious galleries around the world — including the Museum of Modern Art in New York — an impressive collection is held at the Len Lye Centre of the Govett-Brewster Art Gallery in New Plymouth (the first in New Zealand to have a gallery devoted to a single artist).

David Low (1891–1963) was a Dunedin-born artist who became one of the principal and most popular newspaper political cartoonists in the United Kingdom. His damning cartoons of Hitler and Mussolini before and during the Second World War earned him a place in the Nazis' Black Book — a list of those who were to be arrested after the invasion of Great Britain. Winston Churchill said, 'Low is the greatest of our modern cartoonists.' He was knighted in 1962, and *The Guardian* newspaper called him 'the dominant cartoonist of the western world'.

Te Māori was a major touring exhibition of Māori art that opened at New York's Metropolitan Museum of Modern Art in 1984, to great international acclaim.

Writers Keri Hulme and Eleanor Catton have both won the prestigious Booker Prize for Fiction, in Great Britain — Hulme for *The Bone People* in 1984 and Catton for *The Luminaries* in 2013. The latter book received many honours and awards and was made into a BBC/TVNZ mini-series in 2020.

SOME INTERESTING 'FIRSTS'

Mr J. Wrathall opened New Zealand's very first shop on the seafront at Kororāreka (now Russell) in the Bay of Islands, in 1825, selling items, such as tobacco, sugar, cheese, rum, spades, saws, blankets, cutlery, rice and tea.

The very first Christmas in New Zealand was celebrated in 1642 by Abel Tasman and his crew aboard his ship *Heemskerck*. They had pork (with wine) for Christmas dinner.

The first game of rugby played in New Zealand was on May 14th, 1870. Nelson Football Club beat Nelson College 2–0. No tries were scored, it seems.

Although some short documentary films had been made in the early 1900s, New Zealand's first true feature film — in black and white, and silent — was *Hinemoa*, released in 1913. It was directed by French film director Gaston Méliès, brother of George Méliès, who made the famous silent film *A Trip to the Moon* in 1902. New Zealand's first short science-fiction film *A Message from Mars*, directed by Franklyn Barrett, was released in 1903. Unfortunately, neither film has survived, so we'll never know just what that message was!

In 1862, the first railway train ran on a line of 21 kilometres between a copper mine at Dun Mountain to Nelson. The first passenger train was at Christchurch in December, 1863, connecting the city with the port at Ferrymead. By 1867, the line had reached Lyttelton.

The first coconut and banana plants in New Zealand were brought here by early Māori settlers, but they failed to thrive in our cooler climate.

The first New Zealand-produced hit record was 'Blue Smoke' in 1949, written by Ruru Karaitiana, and sung by Pixie Williams. It was top of the radio hit parade for six weeks and sold 20,000 copies in its first year.

The New Zealand Gazette — New Zealand's first newspaper, comprising just four pages — was printed and published in April, 1840. Its name changed several times in the first year — and at one point became *The New Zealand Gazette and Britannia Observer*, as Britannia was the proposed name for the settlement which became Wellington. It ceased publication in 1844.

The first motor cars arrived in New Zealand in 1899. Engineer and cycle mechanic Mr F. L. Dennison decided to build one for himself. A first attempt was a gasoline-powered tricycle (described in a newspaper as 'an ordinary packing case placed on three wheels'), which he drove around Christchurch one evening, and this was followed by the construction of a four-wheeled version in 1900 — our very first New Zealand-built motor car!

He took it for a 500-kilometre spin to Oamaru and back, and had only one breakdown — at Ashburton — which was quickly repaired.

Northland saw a whole heap of New Zealand 'firsts'. Oranges were first planted in 1818, at Kerikeri, and two years later Kerikeri saw the first plough being used. The first bridge — 18 metres long — was built across the Waitangi River in 1830, and the same year the first road was built between Kerikeri and Waimate North. The first church was built in 1823 at Paihia, where the first printing press began operation in 1835.

Captain Cook's crew brewed the first New Zealand beer at Dusky Sound in 1773. It was made from yeast, molasses and leaves from rimu and mānuka trees. Our first winery — the Mission Vineyard, in Hawke's Bay — was established in 1865, and it's still going strong!

To make bread, flour is needed. To get flour, wheat needs to be grown.

French explorer Marion du Fresne grew some wheat on Moturoa Island in 1772, but the first proper wheat crop in New Zealand was grown by the Bay of Islands chief Ruatara, in 1813. When the crop was harvested, he made New Zealand's first loaf of bread — in a frying pan! Today paraoa parai, or fried bread, is still a delicious treat enjoyed by many Kiwis.

Māori have a long history of building river- and sea-going vessels. But the first effort by Europeans came in 1793 in Dusky Sound, when a sealing party attempted to build a sailing ship of about 60 tonnes, but abandoned the effort. The half-built vessel was found two years later by the crew of the damaged *Endeavour* (not Cook's ship — just the same name), who completed the job and rigged it as a schooner. They named the ship *Providence* and with 90 men on board, managed to sail her to Norfolk Island in twelve days.

In December, 1903, the Wright Brothers were the first in the world to achieve powered and controlled flight. In Temuka in the South Island Richard Pearse also achieved powered flight at some point in 1903–1904 (no-one's exactly sure when) although with little control. He flew several hundred metres before crashing into a high hedge — our first aeroplane flight. He'd actually achieved the same results — 'only a few hops' he described it — back in 1901. What makes his achievement even more remarkable is that he made most of the aeroplane's parts himself, working alone on his small farm — adapting bits and pieces of farm machinery, including making the cylinders for the engine from cast-iron drainpipes!

Alarmed at the amount of lawlessness in the Bay of Islands, concerned residents formed the armed Kororāreka Association in 1838, and established New Zealand's first jail, which was made out of a very large sea chest, with air holes drilled in the sides to allow the imprisoned offender some fresh air while incarcerated.

A horse-drawn carriage was New Zealand's first school 'bus' — in Tauranga, in 1924. The first motor school bus started service later that same year, in Piopio.

Although there had been travelling circuses and private animal menageries during the later 1800s, it wasn't until 1906 that New Zealand's first public zoo was opened, in Wellington. In the beginning it had only a single resident — a lion named 'King Dick' — which had been donated by Prime Minister Richard Seddon. The lion was later joined by a kiwi, an emu and a few monkeys.

The Four Square shops opened in the 1920s — our very first grocery cooperatives. However, it wasn't until 1948 that the first self-service grocery store (featuring shopping aisles and baskets so customers could select items themselves) opened — a Four Square grocery store in Onehunga, Auckland. In 1958, Auckland saw the first Foodtown supermarket open in Ōtāhuhu — with parking for 118 cars!

In 1963, our first shopping mall — LynnMall, in Auckland — was opened, and it's still going strong. Our nation's largest shopping mall is at Sylvia Park, Auckland — a retail space of over 100,000 square metres (that's way more than 10 football fields!) with about 250 stores . . . and 5000 carparks. And even larger malls are planned for the future!

PEOPLE AND NUMBERS

New Zealand's population is just over 5,100,000.

A recent census shows that we are 70.2 per cent European, 16.5 per cent Māori, 15.1 per cent Asian, 8.1 per cent Pacific Islanders, 1.5 per cent Middle Eastern/Latin American/African and 1.2 per cent Other Ethnicities.

If you counted up those percentages, and those shown below, you'll see that the totals exceed 100% — that's because many people identify with more than one group, and therefore the segments in these pie charts are . . . er, *almost* exact.

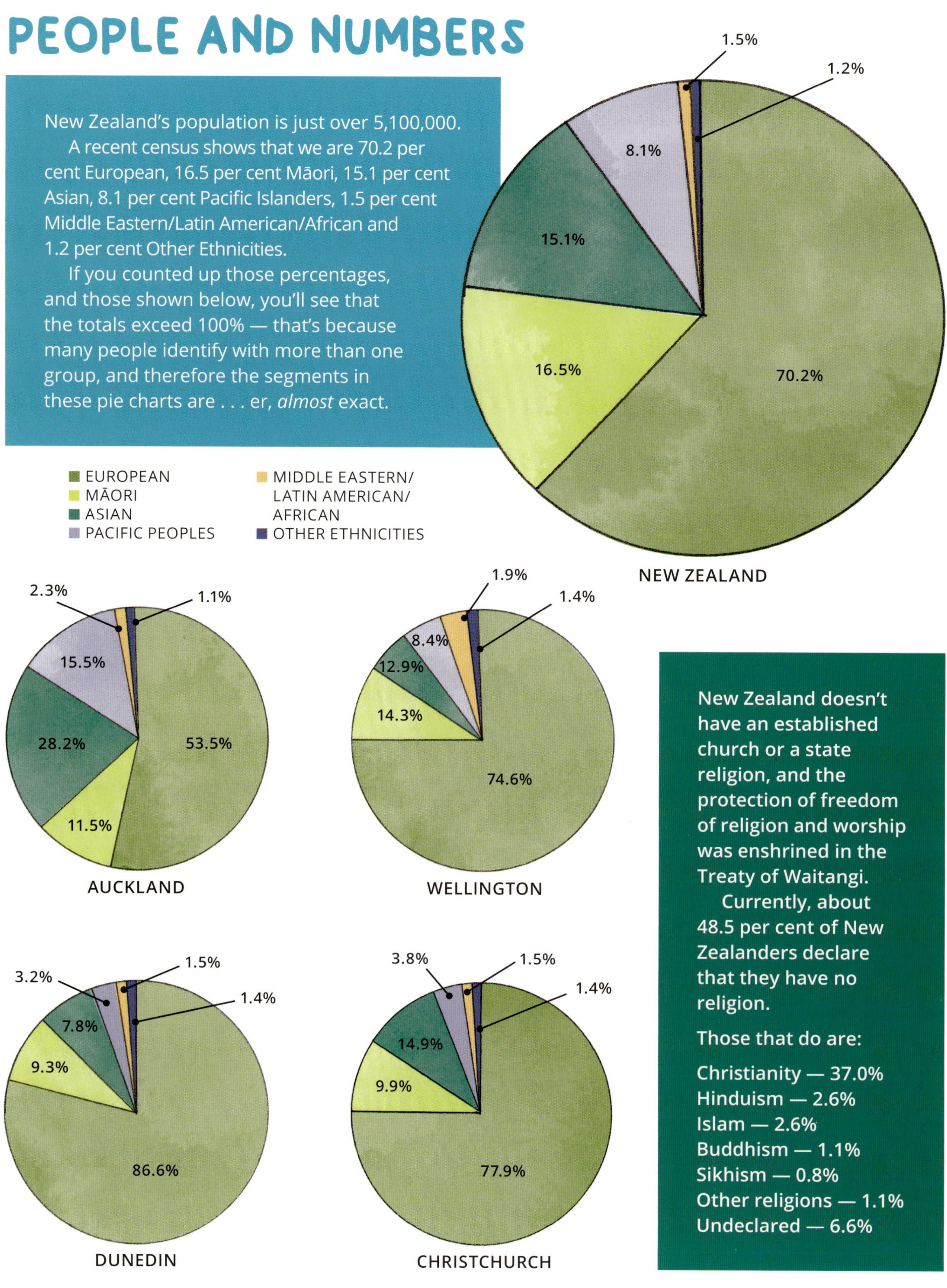

New Zealand doesn't have an established church or a state religion, and the protection of freedom of religion and worship was enshrined in the Treaty of Waitangi.

Currently, about 48.5 per cent of New Zealanders declare that they have no religion.

Those that do are:

Christianity — 37.0%
Hinduism — 2.6%
Islam — 2.6%
Buddhism — 1.1%
Sikhism — 0.8%
Other religions — 1.1%
Undeclared — 6.6%

Over three-quarters of the population lives in the North Island, where our population density is just 18 people per square kilometre. For comparison, Australia's density is 3 (well, most of Australia is just wide-open spaces), Great Britain's population density is 277, the United States is 34, but Macau's (China) density is a whopping 21,055!

The average age of New Zealanders is 37.4 years — 36.7 years for males, and 38.7 years for females. And there are more women than men — for every 100 females, there are 96.66 males (what does 0.66 of a man look like, I wonder?).

Life expectancy in New Zealand is 80 years for males, and 83.5 years for females.

New Zealand has three official languages — English (principally spoken by 95 per cent), Māori (4 per cent) and the New Zealand Sign Language (less than 1 per cent). Having the status of an official language means that any New Zealand citizen can freely choose to use any of the three in formal proceedings, such as in courts and so on.

About 19.5 per cent of our population is aged 0–14 years, 33 per cent aged 15–39 years, 31 per cent aged 40–64 years and 16.5% aged 65 years and over.

The top ten cities, by population.

1. Auckland — 1,463,000
2. Christchurch — 380,600
3. Wellington — 215,900
4. Hamilton — 178,500
5. Tauranga — 155,200
6. Lower Hutt — 111,800
7. Dunedin — 105,000
8. Palmerston North — 81,500
9. Napier — 66,700
10. Porirua — 60,500

New Zealanders buy almost 5,000,000 books per year — one of the highest rates in the world. Although about 400,000 of us claim not to have read a book in a twelve-month period, the rest of us read an average of 20.6 books in a year.

80 per cent of New Zealanders prefer to read a physical book, and 5 per cent prefer a digital e-book. A further 14 per cent are happy to read in both formats.

97 per cent of New Zealand households have at least one television, and about 92 per cent of us watch an average of 20.5 hours of television each week.

94 per cent of the population has full internet access, and 52 per cent of us use the internet to purchase groceries, appliances and clothing and so on . . . oh, and smartphones — over 80 per cent of us have one of those.

We purchase over 150,000 cars each year, and 92.1 per cent of households have at least one car — 37.6 per cent are one-car households, 38.4 per cent are two-car households and 16.1 per cent of households have three cars or more.

Men drive about 12,000 kilometres each year, and women drive about 8000 kilometres. 15 per cent of women aged over 65 have never driven a vehicle, and about 2 per cent of men in this age group have never driven.

Before Covid-19 interrupted our daily lives, about 72 per cent of us travelled for leisure within New Zealand each year — 90 per cent by car, the rest by air, rail and sea.

We made 45 million domestic trips — 61 per cent day trips, and 39 per cent overnight trips.

Half of all households have a bicycle, and about 30 per cent of the population rides a bicycle annually — for a total of 78 million trips by bicycle each year in New Zealand.

Over 600,000 units of whiteware are sold in Aotearoa each year — that's ovens, washing machines, dishwashers, refrigerators and so on. Each unit can cost anything between $1000–$8000.

Kiwis spend anywhere between $400–$700 million each month on furniture, electrical and hardware goods.

Over $170 million is spent in pharmacies/chemists each year, with another $63 million on other medical costs.

Cosmetics sales are nearly $150 million each year, and optical goods sales amount to over $40 million.

We spend about $790 million each year on our pet dogs, at an average cost per household of over $1600. Even though there are more cats than dogs, the bill is cheaper — we spend about $740 million on cats, with a yearly household average of around $1000.

We have nearly 600,000 pet birds (including small private flocks of chickens). The annual spend is $65 million, with a household cost of $500 each year.

Pet rabbits number 116,000 which averages about two per household, and have a yearly cost of $36 million. Just over $200 yearly for each household.

And then there's fish. Lots of them; over 1.5 million fish in tanks and aquariums around the country — and plenty more in garden ponds, too. We spend about $38 million keeping them buoyant, which is just over $204 each year.

Here's a list of a few odd, but interesting 'populations' in New Zealand — but remember some of their numbers can change quite a lot from year to year:

4 Metropolitan zoos
4 International airports
6 Container ports
8 Universities
13 National parks
62 Airports
75 Surf lifesaving clubs
79 Fire stations
(plus 360 volunteer stations)
300 Public libraries
330 Police stations
360 Gyms
500 Railway engines
600 Rugby clubs
1400 Railway stations
1570 Pubs and bars
2536 Schools
4200 Bridges
35,367 Retail premises, including . . .
4000 Dairies and convenience stores, and . . .
900 Pharmacies . . . and
1300 Petrol stations.
49,530 Farms
66,000 Goats
120,000 Horses
234,000 Pigs (French explorer De Surville gave the first two pigs to Northland Māori at Doubtless Bay in 1769)
580,000 Dogs
830,000 Deer
960,000 Private boats
1,300,000 Cats
1,800,000 Dwellings
3,900,000 Cattle
(Dairy cattle produce about 15 billion litres of milk each year!)
4,400,000 Motor vehicles in all categories.
27,000,000 Sheep (the very first sheep were brought here by Captain Cook, in 1773 and 1777)
118,000,000 Chickens
(But how many eggs?)

And here are a few occupations — these numbers too, can vary quite a lot from year to year:
Doctors: 18,258 **Nurses:** 58,206 **Dentists:** 3336
Opticians: 933 **Veterinarians:** 1271
Firefighters: 1700 professionals, plus 8000 volunteers
Police: 9800 officers, plus 3000 other staff
Army: 9778 full-time, plus 2818 reserves
Navy: 2268 full-time and 543 part-time
Air Force: 2516 full-time and 318 reserves
Coastguard: 23 staff and 2235 volunteers
School teachers: 72,000 **Architects:** 1670
Surf lifeguards: 4500 volunteers
NZ Post workers: 4778 **Members of parliament:** 120
Electricians: 13,000 **Painters/Decorators:** 12,300
Plumbers: 8000 **Roofers:** 3696 **Carpenters:** 14,500
Zombies: 0 **IT workers:** 114,000
Forestry workers: 20,000
Authors and Illustrators: Too Many
Fishery workers: 15,500

About 250,000 Kiwis play golf on any of 385 golf courses each year, at least 140,000 play netball (and thousands more in schools) and there are over 128,000 club members and casual players of lawn bowls at 460 clubs. There are nearly 147,000 registered rugby union players . . . and over 2300 referees! There are 150,000 registered football (soccer) players, and over 60,000 children playing junior football.

KIWIANA

So what's Kiwiana all about? Well, it's everything that says, 'Aotearoa New Zealand' . . . heaps of stuff that's uniquely all about 'us'. It's everywhere, and in our daily lives, whether we realise it or not. From food and clothes, to sports and music . . . even in the way we talk! There's plenty of it elsewhere in this book, too . . . like the silver fern (see page 20) and the koru (see page 33).

The people of Otorohanga in the Waikato decided to rename the town 'Kiwiana Town' in 1999 to encourage more tourism — it was already well known for its Kiwi House where tourists could see kiwi in their natural environment. The idea has grown, and now the town holds the Great Kiwiana Festival and special events. With lots of Kiwiana murals and cut-out models around the streets, it's the self-styled 'Kiwiana Capital of New Zealand'.

Yates Garden Guide and the *Edmonds Cookery Book* are two of the biggest-selling books ever published in New Zealand. The Yates seeds and gardening equipment company was founded in 1879, and just six years later published the first *Yates Garden Guide*. There have been nearly 80 editions of the book, and well over a million copies have been sold.

The *Edmonds Cookery Book* has sold over three million copies through 60 editions since it was first published as *The Sure to Rise Cookery Book* in 1908. One edition racked up sales of 200,000 in a single year — making it New Zealand's fastest-selling book!

Lemon and Paeroa — or simply L&P — has been one of the most popular soft drinks in the country for many years. For a long time, residents and visitors to Paeroa enjoyed the waters from its natural mineral springs — filling bottles to take home, and then often adding lemon juice. Due to increasing popularity and demand, The Paeroa Natural Mineral Water Company was established in 1910, and initially sold the drink as Paeroa and Lemon. Over time, the name became Lemon and Paeroa and then became known as just L&P. Even though its recent marketing campaign stated that L&P is 'World Famous in New Zealand' it's also very popular overseas, especially in Australia and Great Britain.

A recent poll showed New Zealanders' current favourite ice-cream flavours:

1. Berry (strawberry, raspberry or boysenberry) 15%
2. Chocolate 13%
3. Vanilla 11%
4. Hokey Pokey 10%
5. Cookies and Cream 9%
6. Salted Caramel 9%
7. Goody Goody Gum Drops 6%
8. Mint Chocolate Chip 5%
9. Rum and Raisin 5%
10. Orange Chocolate Chip 4%
11. Neapolitan 3%
12. Others 10%

HOKEY POKEY ICE-CREAM

The name hokey pokey came from an old-fashioned term for ice-cream vendors, who were known as hokey pokey men. There have been many different versions of ice cream containing small pieces of toffee over the years in New Zealand, but the Tip Top company created the best version — the one we know today. The original recipe was created in the 1950s, and in the 1980s there was a slight recipe change, when honeycomb toffee replaced the solid toffee pieces.

New flavours appear all the time, but hokey pokey still manages to be one of the top-selling ice-cream flavours.

The Buzzy Bee pull-along toy began life in the 1930s. It's had many alterations in its design over the years — some wooden parts replaced with plastic, and colour changes — but its clacking sound and whirling wings have always appealed to small children. Buzzy Bee has featured in picture books, television shows, jigsaws, children's rides, on t-shirts . . . and there's even a Buzzy Bee soft cuddly toy.

In New Zealand we consume more than 40 million litres of ice cream every year — more per person (10–20 litres each) than any other country!

How often do we eat ice cream?

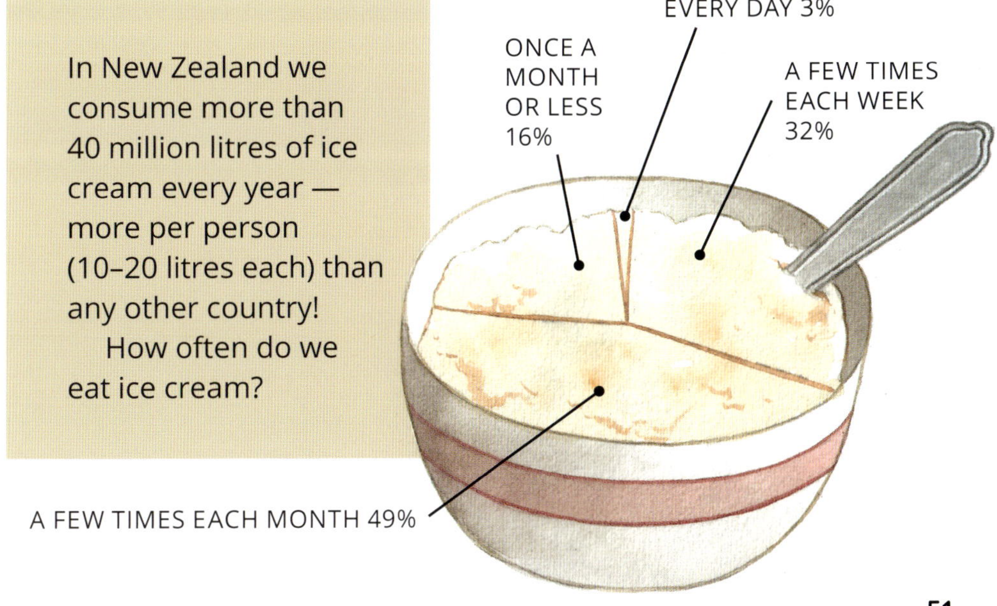

Kiwi Shoe Polish was first produced in 1906 — in Australia! Its creator William Ramsay called it 'Kiwi' in honour of his New Zealand-born wife Annie. It was initially intended as a polish for farmers, to help protect their boots and other leather gear, but it soon gained widespread popularity — and was widely used by British and American forces in the First World War. Its name helped to spread the idea of New Zealanders being known as Kiwis. It's now sold in over 180 countries, and accounts for more than half of all shoe polish sales throughout the world. How many tins are in *your* house?

And we shouldn't forget the Silver Fern — it's a symbol that's been used by the military, airlines, heaps of sportspeople such as the All Blacks, in advertising, on farm products, in fashions and on flags (see pages 20–21). In sport, it was first used on the shirts of the New Zealand Native football team which toured Great Britain in 1888–89. Along with the kiwi, it's one of our most common national symbols.

Giant objects

It seems that half the towns in the country want to have a giant *something* next to the road into town. Look at this weird list:

Paeroa has had a 7-metre-high bottle of L&P (Lemon and Paeroa) since 1968.

Cromwell has had a 13-metre-high selection of fruit since 1989.

Gore has had a 6.5-metre trout since 1989, but it's dwarfed by Rakaia's 12-metre salmon, built two years later (it weighs 1 tonne!).

There's a giant shearer at Te Kuiti, giant gumboots in Taihape, monster crayfish in Kaikoura, a giant bull at Bulls (well, where else?), a huge bicycle in Taupō, a supersized kiwifruit at Te Puke — you can even go inside it and climb the stairs to a viewing platform! Riverton has a 4-metre pāua shell, there's a huge takahē at Te Anau, a giant surfer at Colac Bay, and there's a huge black sandfly at Pukekura.

And right down at the bottom of the South Island, the wee town of Tuatapere has a huge statue of a sausage on a fork!

And — oh yes — there's a *The Simpsons* giant pink doughnut in Springfield, too.

But perhaps the most iconic of all these is the giant 7.5-metre carrot at Ohakune, erected in 1984.

The kiwifruit was introduced to Aotearoa from China in the 1930s, and has now become our biggest fruit export — in 2020, kiwifruit exports totalled 2.5 billion dollars. It's become part of our own lives in a big way, as an addition to breakfasts, drinks, salads, as pavlova toppings, or just cut in half and eaten with a spoon.

The kiwifruit was originally called Chinese gooseberry and for a while melonette was considered as a new branding for the fruit. Fortunately, kiwifruit became its official name in 1959 — firmly establishing its New Zealand identity.

In many countries, it's called simply kiwi and in Taiwan and Hong Kong kiwifruit is sold as strange fruit, as that's the Chinese translation of the name.

Anzac biscuits first appeared as a means of raising funds for the war effort during the First World War, with the tasty treats sold at public events and gatherings. The name Anzac comes from the Australian and New Zealand Army Corps. They were originally called Rolled Oats Biscuits in a 1917 cookery book, but the name Anzac Biscuits soon took over. They've remained one of the most popular biscuits in Australia and New Zealand ever since.

They're simple and easy to make, and here's the recipe — from the *Edmonds Cookery Book* (see page 50) — so that you can make some for yourself!

ANZAC BISCUIT RECIPE

You'll need:
100 g butter
2 tablespoons golden syrup
1/2 cup granulated sugar
1/4 cup brown sugar
1 cup rolled oats
1 cup desiccated coconut
1 cup flour
3/4 teaspoon baking soda
2 tablespoons warm water

1. Preheat the oven to 180ºC.
2. Add butter and golden syrup to a medium-sized saucepan and melt over a medium heat.
3. Add sugars, oats, coconut and flour and mix together.
4. In a small bowl, mix together the baking soda and warm water — add to the pan and combine.
5. Roll the dough into balls about 1 tablespoon in size and place — flattened — onto a lined baking tray.
6. Bake for about 10–12 minutes until the biscuits are golden brown.
7. Allow to cool for about 5 minutes, then transfer to a cooling rack.

There isn't a dessert that's more Kiwiana than pavlova. The dish was created in honour of the Russian ballerina Anna Pavlova, who toured New Zealand and Australia in 1926.

There have been plenty of arguments about which country — New Zealand or Australia — invented the sweet meringue cake, and there was even a theory that it was created in the USA, from a simpler German recipe. Despite all this debate, it was eventually proven that the first-known recipe for pavlova was published in New Zealand — so it's ours!

SOME ODD BITS AND PIECES

There are about 4200 road bridges and about 1700 railway bridges, plus thousands of large and small culverts — it would be a bit difficult to call them true bridges.

The longest road bridge is the Rakaia River Bridge — 1.757 kilometres in length — and right next door, but slightly shorter, is the longest rail bridge.

It's claimed that there are about 800,000 kilometres of farm fencing in New Zealand — that's more than enough to reach to the moon and back!

New Zealand's longest rail tunnel is the Kaimai Tunnel, from Apata to Tauranga — 8.879 kilometres in length. The longest road tunnel is the Waterview Tunnel, in Auckland, at 2.4 kilometres.

Wellington is the southernmost of all the world's capital cities.

There's a total of 94,000 kilometres of roads in New Zealand (state highways and local roads) — that's more than twice around the world. And if you could drive on all of them at 100 kilometres an hour non-stop, it would take 39 days to do it!

While working at the Wellington Post Office, entomologist and astronomer George Hudson wrote a paper proposing the introduction of a system of daylight saving time — moving clocks forward or back according to the change in seasons. Germany and Austria were the first countries to adopt the idea, in 1926. New Zealand followed suit in 1927, and then most of the rest of the world caught on to the idea.

At 10,000 square metres, Wellington's Old Government Building is the largest wooden building in the Southern Hemisphere, and one of the largest in the world. It was made of kauri in a style that mimicked Italian stone palaces. It opened in 1876, and in the same year became the first building in the world to have a smoke-free policy, to safeguard it against fire. It's over 76 metres long, has 530 doors, 143 rooms, 126 fireplaces, 64 toilets and 22 chimneys . . . plus 804 windows!

Canterbury settlers introduced hedgehogs to the country in 1870 — and now there are more of them in New Zealand than there are in Great Britain!

The official centre of New Zealand is at Nelson's Botanical Hill.

The steepest street in the world — at a gradient of 1:2.86 — is Dunedin's Baldwin Street. In some parts it's as steep as 1:1!

Colin Murdoch, of Christchurch, was the inventor of the disposable plastic syringe, now used in their millions all around the world every day. Before his invention, glass syringes — and even newer plastic ones — had to be laboriously cleaned and sterilised between uses. He also invented the tranquilliser gun, used to safely subdue animals.

The Kaipara Harbour can claim to be the largest in the world, but because it's comprised mostly of low-lying estuaries, the claim's only really valid when the tide is in!

It stretches 60 kilometres from north to south, and covers 947 square kilometres. The ins and outs of its many arms measures 3000 kilometres! Deeper and more fully navigable harbours, such as Sydney Harbour and Falmouth Harbour in England also claim to be the biggest in the world, but they still can't compare to the Kaipara when it's at its very best!

There are about 4100 kilometres of railway lines in New Zealand, and over 500 kilometres of that is able to be used by electric trains.

A recent Canstar survey has discovered the most popular individual pies in New Zealand. The winner is mince and cheese, with 22 per cent of the population rating it the top pie. As a nation, we consume about 15 pies per person per year — that's over 74 million pies annually!

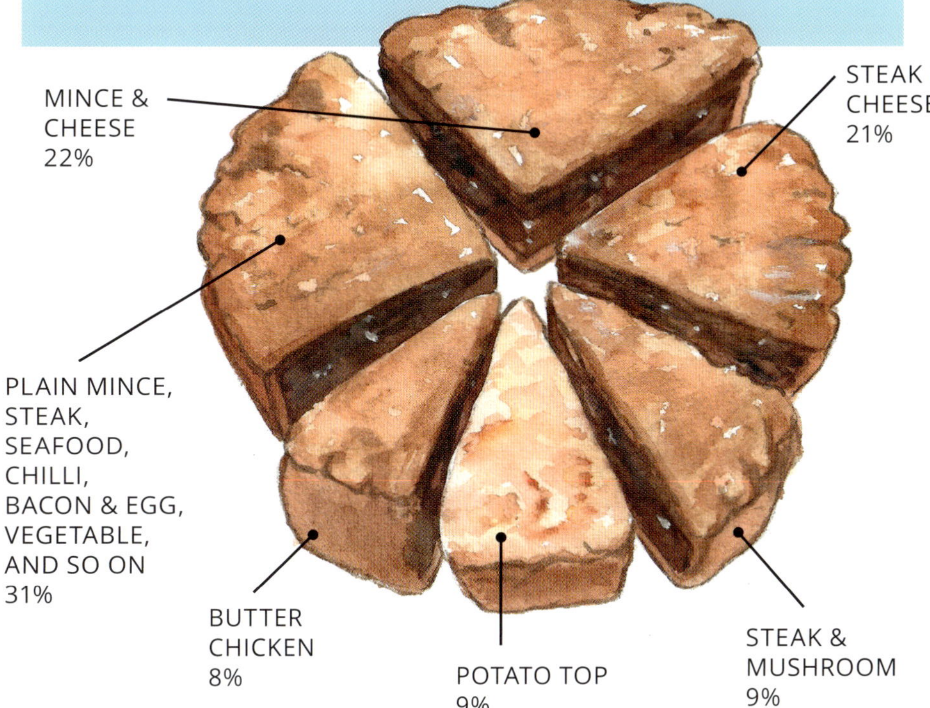

The oldest wooden building in New Zealand is Kemp House at Kerikeri — built in 1822. And just next door is the oldest stone building — the Stone Store, built in 1835.

Horticulture — the growing of crops, such as fruit and vegetables — takes up about 1252 square kilometres of land. Our largest single vegetable crop is potatoes, at about 94 square kilometres, and our largest fruit crop is wine grapes, at 340 square kilometres. However, dairy farming takes up well over 17,000 square kilometres of our land — that's an area about 28 times the size of Lake Taupō!

New Zealand's smallest church was built at Doubtless Bay, Northland, in 1861, and moved to a Whangarei Museum in 1946. Made from a single kauri tree, it could hold a congregation of just 20 people.

The Chatham Islands observe their own individual time zone, which is 45 minutes ahead of the rest of New Zealand.

NEW ZEALAND TIMELINE

Some of the following entries have been covered earlier in the book, but they're included here to show how everything fits together and progresses through time.

1100–1400 First Māori settlers arrive.

1642 Abel Tasman becomes the first European to see New Zealand.

1769 Captain James Cook becomes the second.

1772 Marion du Fresne arrives in Aotearoa, but outstays his welcome in the Bay of Islands, and is killed, along with 24 of his crew. In reprisals, 250 Māori are killed or wounded.

1773 Captain Cook releases the first sheep in New Zealand, at Dusky Sound, but a few days later they die from eating poisonous plants. He releases the first European birds — five geese — and calls the place Goose Cove. His crew also take the time to brew New Zealand's first beer.

1794 The country's first kauri logging operation is established on Great Barrier Island.

1802 European sealing stations are established.

1806 Moehanga (Te Mahanga) of Ngāpuhi is the first Māori to travel to England, where he claims to have met King George III and Queen Charlotte. He returns in 1807.

1806 First Pākehā women arrive in New Zealand.

1815 First Pākehā born in New Zealand — Thomas Holloway King, at Rangihoua.

1819 First grapevines are planted by Samuel Marsden at Kerikeri. However, due to poor fencing, the local goats have a feed and destroy the growing vines.

1820 The first European-style plough is put to use at Kerikeri.

1823 Phillip Tapsell marries Maria Ringa, in the Bay of Islands — the first Church of England wedding in New Zealand.

1831 Whaling stations are established in the Tory Channel and at Preservation Inlet.

1832 New Zealand's first cricket match is played by Māori and Pākehā pupils at Samuel Marsden's Mission School in the Bay of Islands.

1834 The United Tribes of New Zealand flag is adopted.

1834 William Colenso brings a printing press to New Zealand and produces publications in te reo Māori. He later prints the Treaty of Waitangi in Māori.

1835 Charles Darwin visits the Bay of Islands during his explorations on HMS *Beagle*.

1839 Mary Bumby introduces honeybees to New Zealand, near Hokianga Harbour. By the 1860s, local Māori have become the country's first commercial beekeepers.

1840 Māori population is estimated to be around 80,000. Pākehā number about 2000.

1840 Treaty of Waitangi is signed.

1840 New Zealand's first newspaper is published — *The New Zealand Gazette*.

1840 Okiato (Old Russell) becomes the nation's capital.

1840 A small French colony is established at Akaroa, and it is named Port Louis-Philippe.

1841 The nation's capital moves to Auckland.

1842 The first Anniversary Day Regatta is held in Auckland.

1842 The very first A&P show is held in the Bay of Islands.

1843 22 European settlers and 4 Māori are killed at the Wairau River, in Marlborough. Generally acknowledged as the start of the New Zealand wars.

1846 The first steam vessel seen in New Zealand — HMS *Driver*, a six-gun paddle-driven sloop — arrives as part of her circumnavigation of the world; the first steam vessel to achieve the feat.

1847 First public hospital is established, in Wellington.

1847 Auckland Savings Bank (ASB) opens for business.

1848 First Scottish settlers arrive in Otago.

1849 First coal — half a tonne — is mined at Taupiri, near Huntly.

1850 First stagecoach service established, in the South Island.

1853 New Zealand's first general election is held — it takes over two months to count the votes from all around the country.

1854 The first volunteer fire-fighting brigade is formed, in Auckland.

1855 Wairarapa/Wellington earthquake.

1855 New Zealand issues its own postage stamps for the first time.

1856 Nelson College — the country's first state secondary school — opens its doors with a roll of just eight boys.

1858 Nelson becomes the first township to be given city status.

1858 At Riverton, in Southland, possums are released in the hope of starting a trade in fur and skins. (Didn't turn out so well, did it?)

1858 Te Wherowhero is crowned the first Māori king, and takes the name Pōtatau I.

1859 Gold is discovered in the Buller River.

1859 Pencarrow Head — our first permanent lighthouse — begins operation under lighthouse keeper Mary Bennett, the only woman to ever hold this post in New Zealand.

1860 European population in New Zealand reaches 100,000. Māori population is thought to be about 60,000 at this time, down from 90,000 in the late 1700s.

1860 First oil wells drilled, in Taranaki.

1860 Tāwhiao succeeds his father Pōtatau as Māori king.

1861 Over 6000 buildings completed in Auckland by this time.

1861 Gold is discovered at Gabriel's Gully, beginning the Otago gold rush.

1862 Horse-drawn trams are introduced in Nelson.

1862 First shipment of gold is transported — from Dunedin to London.

1862 First professional opera performance, by the English Opera Troupe, at Dunedin.

1863 First public railway in New Zealand, between Christchurch and Ferrymead.

1863 New Zealand's greatest maritime disaster occurs; HMS *Orpheus* sinks in the Manukau Harbour, with the loss of 189 lives.

1865 The nation's capital moves from Auckland to Wellington.

1865 Gas street lighting installed in Auckland.

1866 The first telegraphic cable is laid under Cook Strait to connect the North and South islands.

1868 First Māori members of parliament are elected.

1868 New Zealand is the first in the world to establish a single standard time throughout the country.

1869 The country's first university — Otago — is founded.

1870 Pākehā population reaches 300,000.

1870 First game of rugby is played, in Nelson.

1871 Steam trams are introduced, in Thames.

1871 Deer are released in Otago.

1872 First entirely New Zealand-built steam locomotive, at Dunedin.

1877 Kate Edger is the first woman to earn a degree at a New Zealand university, and the first woman in the British Empire with a Bachelor of Arts degree (BA).

1881 Telephone exchanges are established in Auckland and Christchurch.

1881 The Dunedin Cable Tramway begins operations (the second in the world after San Francisco). It closed in 1957.

1882 First shipment of frozen meat leaves Port Chalmers for England.

1884 New Zealand's first public art gallery opens, in Dunedin.

1884 First overseas tour by the New Zealand rugby team — to New South Wales.

1885 First New Zealand export of butter (two barrels of salted Eltham butter) to Great Britain.

1886 Mount Tarawera erupts, destroying the world-famous Pink and White Terraces. Approximately 120 people died.

1886 Anchor butter is launched.

1888 The first visit by an overseas rugby team, a private tour by British players, who play 17 games against provincial sides.

1888 The silver fern is used as a national symbol for the first time, by the New Zealand rugby team.

1888 Reefton, in the South Island, becomes the first town to have a public electricity supply.

1890 Aucklander 'Torpedo Billy' Murphy wins the world featherweight boxing title, in San Francisco.

1891 First tamarillos (tree tomatoes) grown in New Zealand.

1891 Bob Fitzsimmons wins the world middleweight boxing title, in New Orleans.

1892 The New Zealand Rugby Football Union is founded.

1892 The Wellington and Manawatu Railways locomotive No.10 establishes a world speed record for narrow-gauge operation — reaching a speed of 103 kilometres per hour.

1892 The Atalanta Cycling Club in Christchurch is the first cycling club for women in Australasia.

1893 Āpirana Turupa Ngata becomes the first Māori university graduate with a Bachelor of Arts, and a Bachelor of Laws degree following in 1897.

1893 New Zealand becomes the first country in the world to give women the vote.

1893 Elizabeth Yates becomes mayor of Onehunga — the first woman mayor in the British Empire.

1894 Our first national park — Tongariro — is officially established. New Zealand now has 13 national parks.

1894 Death of the Māori king Tāwhiao, who is succeeded by his son Mahuta.

1894 On Christmas Day, Tom Fyfe, George Graham and Jack Clarke were the first climbers to reach the top of Mount Cook.

1896 The New Zealand Police Force is established.

1897 New Zealand's first air-mail service is established — by pigeon post between Auckland and Great Barrier Island.

1897 Bob Fitzsimmons wins the world heavyweight boxing title, in Carson City, Nevada.

1897 Margaret Cruickshank qualifies as our first woman doctor, and Ethel Benjamin is the first woman to be admitted as a barrister and solicitor of the Supreme Court of New Zealand.

1898 First public screening of a motion picture — a short film, showing the opening of the Auckland Industrial and Mining Exhibition.

1899–1902 New Zealand troops engage in their first overseas conflict — the Boer War in South Africa.

1900 The first motor-car is built in New Zealand, by Mr F. L. Dennison of Christchurch.

1900 New Zealand's first motor car fatality occurs — a Timaru driver is trapped under her car which went down a bank.

1901 New Zealand is the first country to introduce training for the registration of nurses, and in 1902 Ellen Dougherty becomes the first registered nurse in the world.

1901 Nicholas Oates, of Christchurch, is charged with driving a motor vehicle at a speed greater than 6.5 kilometres an hour (it frightened nearby horses!), and is fined £1 (about $190 today).

1901 New Zealand officially decides not to become a state of Australia.

1902 The current New Zealand flag is officially adopted.

1902 The Wellington Cable Car begins operation, and changes to a funicular system in 1979.

1903–1904 New Zealander Richard Pearse achieves powered flight.

1903 Bob Fitzsimmons wins the world light-heavyweight boxing title, in San Francisco.

1905 New Zealand's rugby team is called the All Blacks for the first time, during their tour of Great Britain.

1906 First New Zealand public zoo is established, in Wellington.

1907 New Zealand becomes a dominion within the British Commonwealth.

1907 The first issue of *The School Journal* is published.

1908 New Zealander Ernest Rutherford is awarded the Nobel Prize in Chemistry for his work in nuclear science and the construction of the atom.

1908 New Zealand's population passes 1,000,000.

1908 The North Island Main Trunk railway is completed — from Wellington to Auckland.

1909 The largest gold nugget ever found is discovered at Ross on the West Coast of Aotearoa. Called the 'Honorable Roddy', it weighed over 3 kilograms. It was presented to King George V as a gift for his coronation. It was later found that it had been melted down to make forks and spoons for the royal dining table!

1910 Freda du Faur becomes the first woman to climb Mt Cook.

1912 The ship *Earnslaw* begins service on Lake Wakatipu.

1914–1918 First World War. About 99,000 New Zealanders serve overseas, with 16,000 killed. New Zealand and Australian troops take part in the Gallipoli campaign, generating the use of the term Anzac (Australian and New Zealand Army Corps).

1918–1919 6700 die in New Zealand's influenza epidemic.

1920 First feijoa grown in New Zealand.

1920 First aeroplane flight across Cook Strait.

1923 First Chatham Cup Final. Seacliff, of Otago, beat Wellington YMCA 4–0.

1926 Ballerina Anna Pavlova gives performances in New Zealand, and three years later the recipe for the dessert named in her honour is first published.

1927 First passionfruit vines are planted, in Kerikeri.

1928 First trans-Tasman flight. Charles Kingsford Smith and crew fly the *Southern Cross* from Sydney to Christchurch in 14.5 hours.

1929 The first 'talking movie' to be shown in New Zealand — *Street Angel* — is shown at the Paramount Theatre in Wellington, and the following year New Zealand's first home-made 'talkie' move — a newsreel — is shown at Auckland's Plaza Theatre.

1930 Chinese gooseberries first grown commercially in New Zealand, and in 1959 are given the name kiwifruit.

1931 256 people are killed in an earthquake in Napier.

1932 First edition of the *New Zealand Woman's Weekly* magazine is published.

1933 First woman MP is elected — Elizabeth McCombs, representing Lyttelton.

1934 The first Farmers Santa Parade, in Auckland.

1936 State housing is introduced.

1936 Jack Lovelock wins gold in the 1500 metres in a world-record time at the Olympic Games in Berlin.

1936 Jean Batten completes a record flight from England to New Zealand.

1937 Free milk introduced in schools.

1938 The first Silver Ferns netball team is formed. They go on to win the world championships five times.

1939 Fisher & Paykel make New Zealand's first locally built washing machines.

1939–1945 Second World War. 140,000 New Zealanders serve overseas, with 12,000 killed. HMNZS *Achilles* plays a vital part in the Battle of the River Plate — engaging the German pocket battleship *Graf Spee*.

1940 The first Y-front men's underwear goes on sale.

1941 HMS *Neptune*, due to be handed over to the New Zealand Navy, and with 150 New Zealanders in its 765 crew, is sunk by mines in the Mediterranean. Only one crew member survives. This book's author lost his Uncle Tommy in the tragedy.

1945 New Zealand signs the charter to establish the United Nations.

1945 Buzzy Bee toy developed.

1945 Main railway line from Christchurch to Picton is completed.

1947 The National Orchestra gives its first performance, at Wellington Town Hall.

1947 Mabel Howard becomes the first woman member of cabinet.

1947 41 people die in a fire at Ballantyne's department store, in Christchurch.

1948 Thought to be long extinct, a small population of takahē is discovered in the South Island's Murchison Mountains.

1949 Compulsory military training begins, later changing to national service, and ends in 1962.

1949 First Māori woman — Iriaka Rātana — is elected to parliament.

1950–1953 Korean War.

1950 Auckland hosts the British Empire Games.

1951 A state of emergency is declared, after a prolonged dispute with waterfront workers.

1952 Waipoua Forest is declared a forest sanctuary, to protect the last major stand of kauri.

1952 New Zealand's population passes 2,000,000.

1953 New Zealander Edmund Hillary and Sherpa Tenzing Norgay reach the summit of Mount Everest.

1953 Queen Elizabeth arrives in New Zealand — the first visit by a reigning monarch.

1953 151 die in the Tangiwai rail disaster.

1954 Bill Hamilton invents the jetboat.

1954 First performance by the New Zealand Opera Group (later Company) in Wellington, which is broadcast live on radio.

1954 New Zealand becomes a member of the United Nations Security Council.

1955 Kawerau, pulp and paper mill opens.

1955 Rimutaka rail tunnel opens.

1956 New Zealand cricket's first test win — defeating the touring West Indies side by 191 runs, at Eden Park.

1957 Scott Base in Antarctica established.

1957 Jandals make their first appearance.

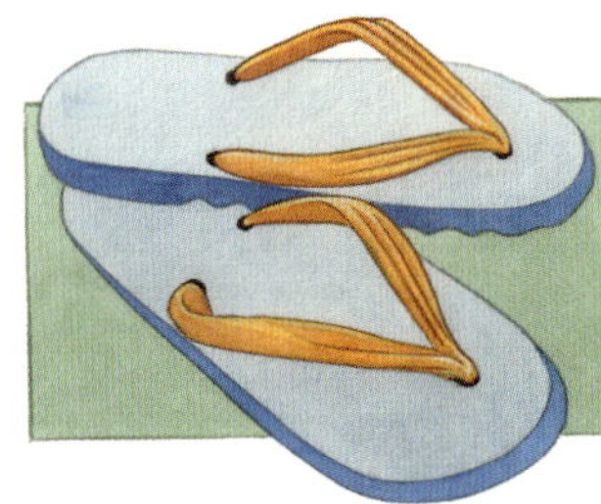

1959 Auckland Harbour Bridge is opened.

1960 Regular television broadcasts begin in Auckland — for just two hours each Wednesday!

1960 New Zealand's first international airport opens in Christchurch.

1962 Cook Strait rail ferry service begins operation.

1963 First shopping mall — LynnMall, in Auckland — opens.

1963–1975 More than 3000 New Zealand military and civilian personnel serve in the Vietnam War.

1964 The Beatles tour New Zealand.

1964 Marsden Oil Refinery, near Whangarei, begins operations.

1964 Lyttelton road tunnel opens.

1965 TEAL becomes Air New Zealand.

1966 Te Atairangi kaahu becomes the first Māori Queen.

1967 New Zealand adopts decimal currency.

1967 The first Moro bars go on sale.

1968 The interisland ferry *Wahine* capsizes and sinks in Wellington Harbour, with the loss of 51 lives.

1969 Glenbrook steel mill begins production.

1969 Breath and blood testing begins, for suspected drunk drivers.

1971 Manapouri Power Station commissioned.

1971 Satellite station at Warkworth begins operation.

1972 The Dunedin–Christchurch night express becomes the last passenger steam train to cease operation.

1973 Colour TV broadcasts begin.

1973 A New Zealand frigate — HMNZS *Otago* — sails to Mururoa to protest against French nuclear testing.

1974 Christchurch hosts the Commonwealth Games.

1975 Lynne Cox becomes the first woman to swim Cook Strait.

1975 The Waitangi Tribunal is established.

1975 Māori land march — led by Whina Cooper, walking from Te Hāpua — reaches Parliament, in Wellington.

1976 New Zealand Day is renamed Waitangi Day.

1976 New Zealand adopts the metric system.

1977 'God Defend New Zealand' replaces 'God Save the Queen' as our national anthem.

1978 The New Zealand Film Commission established.

1979 Air New Zealand sightseeing flight crashes on Mount Erebus in Antarctica, with the loss of 257 lives.

1981 Wellington's 'Beehive' parliament building completed.

1981 South African rugby team's tour of New Zealand meets widespread protests.

1982 First kōhanga reo (full-immersion te reo Māori early-childcare centre) established.

1982 FM radio broadcasts begin.

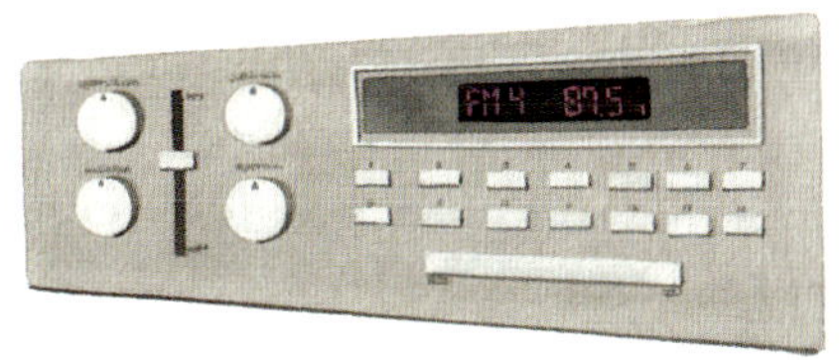

1982 The New Zealand football team compete at their first FIFA World Cup Finals.

1983 Lorraine Downes, from Auckland, wins the Miss Universe title.

1983 This author's first book — *Collins Guide to the New Zealand Seashore* — is published!

1984 *Poi E* by the Pātea Māori Club tops the record charts for four weeks, and is the top-selling record for the year.

1984 *Te Māori* opens as a major exhibition at the New York Metropolitan Museum of Art.

1985 Keri Hulme wins the Booker Prize for her book *The Bone People*.

1985 French agents bomb and sink the Greenpeace vessel *Rainbow Warrior* in Auckland Harbour.

1986 Goods and Services Tax (GST) is introduced.

1986 Pope John Paul II is the first pope to visit New Zealand.

1987 New Zealand wins the first Rugby World Cup, in Auckland.

1987 The first Lotto draw is held.

1987 Māori is made an official language of New Zealand.

1987 First mobile phones appear in New Zealand — many about the size of a brick, costing up to $6000, and with a battery life of just 20 minutes!

1989 Capital punishment is abolished.

1990 Auckland hosts the Commonwealth Games.

1992 Texting technology begins. LOL!

1993 Although the internet had its beginnings in 1983, it wasn't until 1993 that it became widely available to the public.

1994 New Zealand's first casino opens in Christchurch.

1994 The first Big Day Out music festival is held in Auckland.

1995 New Zealand wins the America's Cup in San Diego, USA.

1995 The Auckland Warriors have their first match, but lose to the Brisbane Broncos 22–25.

1995 Pauly Fuemana/OMC has a worldwide number one hit single with 'How Bizarre'.

1996 First general election occurs under MMP.

1997 Auckland's Sky Tower opens.

1998 Te Papa Museum opens, in Wellington.

1998 The national women's rugby team — the Black Ferns — wins the first Women's Rugby World Cup, in The Netherlands. They go on to win the world championships again in 2002, 2006, 2010, 2017 and 2022!

1999 Jenny Shipley (National Party) becomes our first female Prime Minister.

2000 New Zealand successfully defends the America's Cup.

2003 New Zealand's population passes 4,000,000.

2006 Facebook and Twitter begin.

2010 Pike River mine explosion traps and kills 29 miners.

2011 Following a damaging earthquake just four months earlier, Christchurch is devastated by a magnitude 6.3 earthquake, destroying or damaging thousands of buildings and taking 185 lives.

2011 New Zealand wins the Rugby World Cup for the second time, in Auckland.

2014 Eleanor Catton wins the Booker Prize for her book *The Luminaries*.

2015 New Zealand wins the Rugby World Cup for the third time, in London!

2016 Instagram begins.

2017 New Zealand wins the America's Cup again, in Bermuda!

2019 Mosque shootings in Christchurch leave 51 dead.

2019 Whakaari/White Island erupts while tourists are exploring. Twenty-two people are killed and 25 injured.

2020 Covid-19 reaches New Zealand.

2020 New Zealand's population reaches 5,000,000.

2020 New Zealand successfully defends the America's Cup once more!

2021 New Zealand beats India to win the inaugural World Cricket Test Championship, in England.

2022 On the death of Queen Elizabeth II, Charles III becomes King of New Zealand.

2023 This book is published!

INDEX

THE END OF THE BOOK

So here we are at the end. It's usual to have Acknowledgements and For Further Reading at this point, so here goes.

I'm indebted to many government departments and agencies for the helpful information I've used in this book — GNS Science, Department of Conservation, The National Library and NZHistory, Te Ara, Creative New Zealand, the Ministry for the Environment, Ministry of Transport and the Ministry for Culture and Heritage — and many, many other websites — such as Tourism New Zealand and Wikipedia. I'm also grateful for the fascinating and unusual facts and figures published by Statista, Stuff, Nielsen market research, Canstar Blue surveys and especially the Department of Statistics — and of course I also consulted a wide variety of books concerned with New Zealand history and general information.

Thanks also to Edmonds for their Anzac Biscuits recipe — we tried it, and they all turned out lovely!

Special thanks are due to Te Puni Kōkiri — the Ministry of Māori Development — for their advice and notes regarding the ministry's iwi map, and on which my own iwi map (page 11) is based. And perhaps I should be bold and thank myself too, as I've also consulted many of my own previously published books for lots of interesting stuff to update or expand on and include here . . . and I've recycled a few favourite jokes, too! So, thanks Dave!*

As for further reading, there are many excellent publications out there full of great stuff about our country — *New Zealand Geographic* magazine, and *Forest and Bird* for example, and there are many others covering all aspects of life in New Zealand. So, if you want to know more about Aotearoa New Zealand . . . get stuck in.

Dave Gunson

*My pleasure, mate! :)